S0-BYW-865

Dark Light

SUNY series, Alternatives in Psychology
Michael A. Wallach, editor

Dark Light

The Appearance of Death
in Everyday Life

Ronald Schenk

STATE UNIVERSITY OF NEW YORK PRESS

Published by
State University of New York Press, Albany

© 2001 State University of New York

All rights reserved

Printed in the United States of America

No part of this book may be used or reproduced
in any manner whatsoever without written permission.
No part of this book may be stored in a retrieval system
or transmitted in any form or by any means including
electronic, electrostatic, magnetic tape, mechanical,
photocopying, recording, or otherwise without the prior
permission in writing of the publisher.

For information, address State University of New York Press,
90 State Street, Suite 700, Albany, N.Y., 12207

Production by Cathleen Collins
Marketing by Michael Campochiaro

Library of Congress Cataloging in Publication Data

Schenk, Ronald, 1944–
    Dark light : the appearance of death in everyday life / Ronald Schenk.
        p. cm. — (SUNY series, alternatives in psychology)
    Includes bibliographical references and index.
    ISBN 0-7914-4769-3 (alk. paper) — ISBN 0-7914-4770-7 (pbk. : alk. paper)
    1. Death—Psychological aspects.   I. Title.   II. Series.
BF789.D4 S32 2000
150—dc21   00-021340

10 9 8 7 6 5 4 3 2 1

To Scott, who brought me into the world

CONTENTS

FIGURES

ACKNOWLEDGMENTS

This book arises out of my schooling in Dallas in the 1980s in an approach to cultural psychology created from three different sources. James Hillman followed his predecessors, Sigmund Freud and Carl Jung, in their concern for culture and greatly extended the notion that the "unconscious" to be pursued by depth psychology in contemporary life locates itself in the world. The Dallas Institute of Humanities and Culture, to which the first chapter is dedicated, and especially its co-directors of many years, Robert Sardello and Gail Thomas, provided an oasis which brought to the surface several underground streams of thought related to the life of the city and culture and the interface of the humanities and everyday life. The Psychology Department of the University of Dallas and especially Robert Romanyshyn and Robert Kugelman gave to academia a place to learn psychology as a study of soul reflected in many disciplines.

I am indebted to the Jung societies of several cities for giving me an initial receptive space to air the ideas contained in this book: Dallas, Phoenix, Tucson, Houston, Austin, College Station, Nashville, Sante Fe, Mexico City, San Antonio, and Washington, D.C.

I received helpful suggestions from many friends who are published authors, but I am especially grateful for the friendship of Thomas Moore, who continuously gives freely of himself to many like me attempting to traverse the treacherous landscape of the publishing world. I feel particular gratitude to Frederick Turner, Dennis Slattery, and Mihai Spariosu for their initial reading of the manuscript and their helpful suggestions, to Jane Bunker my Acquisitions Editor, to Cathleen Collins the production manager, and to Maria denBoer for her monumental job of copyediting my manuscript.

Finally, I would like to express my love and appreciation to my wife, Charlotte, for her tutoring me in the things of the world.

Permission is gratefully acknowledged for the following:

An earlier version of chapter 1, "Beauty as Healer," was published in the journal, *Psychological Perspectives,* Vol. 19, No. 2, Fall–Winter, 1988, as "Navajo Healing: Aesthetics as Healer."

An earlier version of chapter 3, "Ball/Play: The Soul of Game," was published by Chiron Publications in *Psyche and Sports,* edited by Murray Stein and John Hollwitz, 1994, as "Ball/Play."

An earlier version of chapter 4, "Spirit in the Tube: The Life of Television," was published by Routledge in *Studies in Jungian Phenomenology,* edited by Roger Brooke, 1999, under the same title.

An earlier version of chapter 8, "The Soul of Race/The Heart of Color," was published in the *Journal of Analytic Social Work,* Vol. 5, No. 3, 1998, under the same title.

Viking/Penguin/Grossman for selection from *The Poetics of Reverie* by Gaston Bachelard, translated by Daniel Russell, 1971, in Chapter 2.

W.W. Norton and Random House (for British Commonwealth rights) for selection from *Duino Elegies* by Rainer Maria Rilke, Translation, Introduction and Commentary by J.B. Leishman and Stephen Spender, 1963, in Chapter 3.

Grove Press for selection from *Endgame: A Play in One Act* by Samuel Beckett, 1958, in Chapter 3.

Jerome Agel for Figure 6, "Renaissance Observers" in Chapter 4, from *The Medium is the Massage* by Marshall McLuhan and Quentin Fiore, 1967, Bantam Books.

Associated University Presses for Figures 1–5, in Chapter 4, from *The Soul of Beauty* by Ronald Schenk, 1992.

Random House and Faber and Faber (for British Commonwealth rights) for "The Irish Cliffs of Moher" by Wallace Stevens from *Collected Poems,* 1952, in Chapter 5.

HarperCollins for "Sometimes A Man Stands Up During Supper" in Chapter 5 from *Selected Poems of Rainer Maria Rilke,* edited and translated by Robert Bly, 1981; "Finding the Father," in Chapter 5 and "A Man and a Woman Sit Near Each Other," in Chapter 6 from *Selected Poems* by Robert Bly, 1986, and lines from "Thrush" by Ted Hughes in Chapter 7 (Faber and Faber for world rights).

NOSING THE FACE

An Introduction

In preparing this book for publication, I was reminded of my family's history of attempts at production and salesmanship. My great-grandfather made glue in factories at different locations across the Midwest. His problem was that he could not get any of the factories to stick together. They would fall apart financially, and he would have to move on to another town and start all over again. His son, my grandfather, traveled to schools in the city of Chicago to sell maps. Inevitably he would get lost on the way and had to bring my grandmother along to navigate. Now, while I am writing a book that has to do with beauty and vision, I can hear a voice in the background saying, "But Ron, what about your appearance?!" These family stories illustrate one of the themes of this book: that we are always intending something, seeing our goal in one direction, while encompassed by something else, a larger form, which is working through us with its own intentions.

In rural America there was a tradition of combining entertainment and education in a gathering called the "chautauqua." On these occasions a visiting lecturer would come and give a talk, usually as part of a series of lectures or cultural events given for popular adult education. The lecture would often take place in a tent in conjunction with a local fair or festival.

As we reimagine this situation, we might say that entertainment and ideas go together. The phrase "entertaining ideas" suggests that ideas have a life and desire of their own. The word "entertain" originally meant "to hold in the house." As James Hillman, a contemporary depth psychologist of culture, has suggested, ideas can be entertained by being given a place, listened to, and nurtured as our guests (Hillman 1981). Entertain also means "to hold in between." Ideas themselves are between existence and meaning. The abstract ideal or "spirit" finds its place or home—its "matter"—in the

1

concrete world through ideas, while at the same time the concrete world realizes its dynamic source or meaning—its spirit—through ideas. Existence and meaning, the material and the spiritual, come together or co-constitute each other in the idea (Davidson 1985, 64–65).

We think we have ideas, but from a more encompassing perspective, ideas have us, as if they were tents in which we find ourselves housed. We consider ideas, and etymologically, the word "consider" means to be "with the stars." One of the founders of depth psychology, the Swiss psychiatrist C. G. Jung, talked about ideas as *daimones,* beings sent from heaven to earth. So ideas can be thought of as autonomous, semidivine beings, holding us and at the same time linking us with another realm. The word "idea" has its root in the Greek *eidos,* which refers to "that which can be seen," from which comes the Latin *video,* "to see." So ideas are like videos that can be imaginatively seen as they influence us. We are always characters in one video or another!

The Native American Navajo tribe conducts healing ceremonies in which gods are invited to make their appearance to help in the process. What is healed when we entertain ideas? For the Greeks, *eidos* brought together the spiritual and the material, mind and matter, the unseen and the seen. These are aspects of life that are held separate in our contemporary world. We think of spirit as split off from everyday life into churches, sanctuaries, chapels, and sacred places, while at the same time we think of the world of matter in terms of scientific reality and causal effects. For the Greeks, "seeing" was the action involved in perceiving the *eidolons,* the particles that make up events whether materially present as a thing or spiritually present as a god. We now call this "imagination," something of concrete form that also is spiritual or beyond the literal. In the Greek sense, the action of seeing imaginatively, as we do when we entertain ideas, brings the worlds of spirit and matter together in a kind of healing.

This book is a series of essays connected by the thought that we are encompassed by images or forms in our everyday lives. We usually live instilled with the heroic sense that we are the masters of our fate, that through willful action we experience our potential, and that we are responsible for our own condition. One of the purposes of this book is to temper this attitude and to develop a way of experiencing by imaginatively seeing our lives as formed by ideas that work and play through us.

The experience of loss of control through imaginative perception is subliminally experienced as a kind of death. Jacques Derrida, the contemporary deconstructionist, characterized imagination as a relationship with death ("image is death," Derrida 1974, 184). This sense of death is not literal, of course; rather, it is a metaphor for imagination's undermining, both subtle and overt, of our heroic, ego-oriented attitude toward life.

The book is about culture and imagination—seeing the world through imagination and stimulating our imagination about the world. The title of the introduction, "Nosing the Face," gives an image for knowing the world through imagination. "Nosing" is an allusion to the word *gnosis,* a kind of spiritual knowledge. As David Miller (1981) has shown, it is also an allusion to an intuitive kind of knowing. This knowledge is not a rational understanding gleaned by a distanced, objective eye, but an animal way of knowing as if through sniffing out an unseen essence. Paraphrasing James Joyce, to know the world through direct animal perception is to nose the world.

To come to know the world by seeing is to face the world. At the same time, if the world can be thought of as having a life of its own, it also sees us through its face. The origins of the word "face" tell us that what is seen also sees back as an "other." In this book, the world is thought of as a living being, an "other," which presents itself to us and lives through us in the various aspects of collective life—technology, sports, relationships, violence, and race.

We usually think of life as being within ourselves or within a living plant or animal. We don't think of life as outside in a larger form, even though we refer to exactly this idea in phrases such as "the life of the family" or "the life of the community." These phrases allude to an ancient idea, *anima mundi,* the life of the world, which suggests that a larger soul or life emanates through the things, beings, and events of the world (Hillman 1982a).

From this standpoint, what we call "reality" would be the place of our encounter with the world. Following Plato, we gather the world through our perceptions, while at the same time the world gathers us through its forms. Each moment of consciousness then becomes an existence within an image, like being in a temple where larger forms of spirit meet and encompass our concrete individual particularity.

In sum, this book is about the perception of forms through imagination, and the underlying experience of death that is entailed in imagination. The introductory chapters describe the perception of larger-than-life forms. The first chapter illustrates how beauty—as the alignment of the world with universal forms—works as the central organizing principle of the Navajo culture. The second chapter turns back to the Western tradition and presents the idea that beauty can be seen as a force in the universe that allows for the appearance and being of all things.

Subsequent chapters indicate how the quality of experience of universal forms that show themselves in everyday life is like our usual notion of death. Death works on us without our knowing, as I show in the chapters on ball games and on television-watching. The chapter on sports reveals how the ball game is a ritual of death presenting us with a way of being in which we are played by something larger than our usual sense of self. The next chapter suggests that television is an attempt to draw us "out of our minds" toward a connection with spirit. In this sense, being out of one's mind involves an underlying yearning for death through connection with spirit, bringing relief from an overly burdened subjective sense of self.

Death may also include the experience we associate with depression—sinking down, guilt, loss, and failure—experiences that we habitually encounter in our culture through relationship. The chapters on relationships, couples and father/son, show how our connections with others evoke death as a form or "third body" that encompasses and informs us.

Finally, death is presented as visible in the experience of violence seen as the inevitable appearance of gods as larger forces in our lives and in the threat of "otherness" inherent in racial distinction.

"Soul" is not only currently a popular new age word, but also classically associated with the habitat of the dead, the "underworld," the home of the activated soul. The experience of death is also the experience of soul (Hillman 1979d). The soul exists in the underworld as shade, shadow, or fleeting image where day-world values are turned upside down. In the underworld, goal-oriented action only brings frustration and attempts to control and possess end in failure. Underworld serves as a metaphor throughout this book for the experience of life in-formed by a larger sense of death. The frustration of action allows for the emergence of imagination as the predominant mode of being (Hillman 1979b). While the experience of death is the experience of soul, imagination is the soul's form of expression. This book is an attempt to stimulate our imagination through the evocation of death and the underworld experience, to locate soul in everyday life, to indicate the darker aspect of soul, and to reveal the redeeming quality of this dark light.

PART ONE

Death as Beauty

CHAPTER ONE

Beauty as Healer

Nightly, deep in the heart of the Navajo Reservation, my 2-year-old son falls afoul of fatherly authority at bath time. Taking advantage of every cave and cranny, every nook and covering, every peak and canyon offered by our household furnishings, he conducts guerrilla warfare, exquisitely evading the inevitable frontal march of the great white father, supreme in his cleanliness. One night, after months of carefully plotting countermoves for what I had thought was every conceivable evasive action, I was taken aback to find my renegade adversary circling the house in one sweeping movement, finally coming to rest squarely in front of the gaping tub that patiently awaited its prey. Raising one finger firmly into the air he declared, "Wait! Let's think about what we are doing."

With this psychological move—a move toward interiority, self-reflection, and distance—my son had placed himself squarely into the modern tradition of his Western ancestors. In losing his integral connection with the bath, he forfeited any prior claim he might have had to spiritual kinship with the community of his first two years, Native Americans of the Navajo tribe. The concern of the traditional Navajo is not for consciousness "about" his world, but for consciousness "with" his world.

As a beginner in the field of mental health, I came to the Navajo Reservation in northern Arizona to live and work. I wanted to learn about Navajo healing practices, and especially about the role of archetype, ritual, and symbol. I directed a mental health clinic, and in this capacity, I established associations with medicine men or "singers," attended ceremonies, and talked at length with my Navajo co-workers about traditional healing practices. In the course of this process, and in trying to find a way of relating to the Navajo that was relevant to them, I developed an appreciation for

---

This chapter is dedicated to The Dallas Institute of Humanities and Culture.

the way in which the values and worldview of a culture are reflected in its healing practices. I developed a feeling for the difficulties that arise when one attempts to understand native culture, and I became aware of the role that one's own cultural assumptions play in one's view of other cultures.

Two stories come to mind in highlighting these difficulties. Anthropologist Barbara Tedlock once spoke to a group in Sante Fe about how she went to Guatemala to conduct a study of ethnic music in a native tribe. After several weeks of noninstruction, she asked her informant when they would start talking about tribal music. He answered by handing her a broom. A stay that was to have lasted a few months turned into several years, during which time Barbara and her husband went through rigorous training as initiates into the sorcery native to that tribe. Tedlock did not learn about ethnic music; she learned ethnic music by changing her life.

In the spring of 1983, Alphonso Ortiz, a tribal priest of the Tewa tribe in New Mexico, spoke to a national conference of Jungian psychoanalysts. He remarked on the enthusiasm with which Western people have been drawn to inquire into the lifestyle of Native Americans. Ortiz explained that Native Americans have responded to this phenomenon by selecting certain individuals from the tribe to act as informants to inquiring white people. The selection of the tribal spokesperson is based upon his or her ability to give whites answers that whites want to hear. Ortiz stated that one of these men in fact, was Ochwiay Biano, the Pueblo Indian with whom Jung (1961a) himself had talked and written about in an idealizing manner in a selection often quoted by Jungians.

The Navajo, in particular, have been the subject of this white zeal for information about other cultures. An old joke in anthropology goes: The average Navajo household consists of the father, the mother, the grandparents on the mother's side of the family, the children, and the anthropologist. Perhaps this enthusiasm springs from the white man's recognition of the complexity of Navajo religious life and the degree to which this life is integrally related to practical matters of healing.

In this chapter, I would like to present Navajo culture as founded upon beauty, aesthetics, and the organization of universal forms in alignment with transcendent forces, and in particular, to represent healing as a function of beauty.

"Beauty" as the Navajo Worldview

Culture affects the way psyche reveals itself, and the way in which psyche reveals itself depends upon the "ethos" of the culture. Clifford Geertz (1973,

127) defines a people's ethos as "the tone, character and quality of their life, its moral and aesthetic style and mood; it is the underlying attitude toward themselves and their world that life reflects." The ethos of a particular culture may be said to determine the form of pathology or dysfunction that manifests in that culture. Plague in the Middle Ages, tuberculosis in the Romantic period, and cancer in modern life all reflect the breakdowns particular to Western culture during these periods. Mass guilt is the dark side of the redemptive ethos of the Middle Ages. Infected lungs reflect psyche choked by reason. Cancer is the symptom of a culture gone wild with growth. In this view, body is the manifestation of psyche as interaction between "interior" spirit and "exterior" world. Body as psyche reflects world as psyche.

Just as illness depends upon the shared reality of a culture, so also does treatment. Cultural values and beliefs regarding the nature of causation and health all determine the *form* into which the process of healing is channeled. What works as cure in one culture will not necessarily work in a culture that does not share the worldview out of which that cure emerges. Cure in a culture where disease is seen as caused from within by the proliferation of harmful bacteria will not necessarily be cure in a culture that sees disease as caused from without. Antibiotics and antidepressants, surgery and hormone injections, dances and chants, ritual baths and sandpaintings—all are healing procedures that arise from and are effective within a particular cultural ethos. We will not be able to understand "what heals" in any one culture without first attempting to understand the dominant consciousness or worldview of that culture.

The Navajo worldview is based upon their conception of beauty or *ho'zho'*. Anthropologist Gary Witherspoon explains:

> Beauty is not separated from good, from health, from happiness, or from harmony. Beauty—*ho'zho'*—is a combination of all these conditions. It is not an abstractable quality of things or a fragment of experience; it is the normal pattern of nature and the most desirable form of experience.
>
> For the Navajo, beauty is not so much in the eye of the beholder as it is in the mind of its creator and in the creator's relationship to the created....Beauty is not "out there" in things to be perceived by the perceptive and appreciative viewers, it is a creation of thought. . . . It is not in things so much as it is in the dynamic relationships among things and between man and things. (Witherspoon 1977, 151–58)

Two notions of beauty emerge here which are strange for Westerners. First, beauty—not economics, mechanics or energetics—is the seat of being, the primary mode of organizing experience. Second, beauty is a matter of relationship, not objectivity or subjectivity. Beauty does not lie within an object to be preserved, nor does it lie in the eye of the beholder; it is an "in-between" phenomenon. Sandpaintings, the equivalent of Western master-pieces of art, for example, are destroyed after each ceremony. To the Navajo, the sandpaintings in themselves are not beautiful, rather they create beauty through their healing power. A man ordered a rug of an especially complex pattern on two different occasions from the same weaver. Both rugs came out perfectly, and the weaver remarked to her brother that there must have been something special about the owner. It was understood that the outcome of the rugs was dependent, not so much upon the weaver's skill, but upon the ho'zho' in the owner's life. The quality of his life evoked the beauty in the rugs.

For the Navajo, living in beauty is living in relationship to one's environment—natural surroundings of rocks and water, plants and animals, desert and mountains, and the social milieu of family and community. The traditional Navajo passing a hill will have connection with that hill. He will know it in terms of its place in his own life, its place in tribal history, and its place in Navajo mythology. He will say:

"At this place my family used to stay overnight when we drove the sheep to the winter camp."

"At this place, Kit Carson cut the heads off of nine Navajos and put them on stakes."

"At this place, Monster Slayer arrives to help the patient on his journey in the Nine Night Chant."

For this man, the hill has subjectivity; it is animated in the form of the spirit of the hill. To move the hill or build on it would not only fragment his identity in relationship to it, but it also would disrupt the healing ritual with which the hill is associated. The place is associated with the god and the god is associated with healing. The Navajo does not leave the world through "active imagination" or "guided imagery"; rather, through his imagination he enters into the world. The spirits that he encounters on his healing journey are not spirits of his "unconscious" but spirits of place.

In addition to environment, ho'zho' involves alignment with community. The Navajo strive for social harmony through proper relation to one another. The will of one person or of a group is never forced onto other individuals. Collective action comes about not through majority opinion but through unanimous consent. Everyone must agree before anything is done. The social system is one of clans with an elaborate chain of kinship categories and codes of proper behavior. Traditionally, one jokes with the uncle on the mother's side of the family in a different manner than one jokes with the uncle on the father's side.

In the Navajo world, physical and mental disorders are attributed to wrong or broken alignments with outer life. When one breaks proper connection with community, offends an animal spirit, or has a wrong relation to natural forces (being too near an area where lightning strikes, for example), one becomes susceptible to disease. In accordance with the notion of *ho'zho'* as right connection with outer life, Navajo healing is a public event. The entire family participates in the preparation of the ceremonies, which may last for several days. When a major ceremony occurs, the entire community gathers for the event. For the Navajo, healing of the individual is a healing of the community as well.

"Word" as Speaker, Mover, and Healer

The Navajo language reflects the importance of the interrelationship of entities. It consists not of words in isolation referring to an object or concept, not of subject split from object, but of phrases that describe a certain image or situation. The horse-drinking-water is very different from the horse-being-chased-by-a-dog. It was my experience that Navajo children begin having serious problems with the white educational system in the third grade, when they start learning the syntax of English grammar, which splits the subject from the object.

Navajo language takes us deeper into the differences in orientation of the Navajo and Western worlds. Because Western vision is detached and objectified, we see whatever it is that appears as a referent that is directing us to a source beyond. For us, words are signifiers that point to meaning. We have lost the sense of the entire complex of meaning inherent in the sound of the word itself (Kugler 1982). In contrast, for the Navajo, the sound is the meaning. The same word, given a slightly different intonation, evokes an entirely different image.

The Western concept of symbolism reflects the split in modern consciousness between appearance and meaning. We do not perceive meaning in the very appearance of images but look to a signified referent. Systems of derived meaning, not appearance itself, inform our understanding of the world. The result is a gap between experience and meaning. The traditional

Navajo does not suffer, as Westerners do, from the anxiety that this gap induces. For the Navajo, there is no symbolic representation, no metaphysical move from signifier to signified. For the Navajo the question, "What does it mean?", is itself meaningless. The meaning lies in the appearance of the object or image itself.

The cultural differences regarding the concept of symbolism are reflected in two personal incidents. I was talking to a singer one day and he made mention of his grandfather. I inquired further about his grandfather and the man said, "I have him right here." He then pulled out his pouch of sacred objects and showed me a feather his grandfather had given him. The feather *was* his grandfather just as much as his grandfather's flesh-and-blood being. When the singer paints the god in the sand, it *is* the god. What we call "symbol" is, to the Navajo, the thing itself.

A common design in Navajo artwork looks like a series of steps. When Navajos are asked by Westerners what the design signifies, the reply is that it *is* the mesa. We interpret this response to mean, "This is a symbolic representation of the mesa." Our image of the mesa is an abstraction from a bird's-eye view. For us, the mesa is like a table with only one level. We do not see it in the same way the Navajo do, with what Beaudelaire called the "intimate eye." I stopped my car one day by the side of the road and got out to look at a mesa—and there they were, the steps, just like in the design. From the perspective of the earth itself, the juttings-out of one mesa look like different levels of steps. For the Navajo the image is the reality.

In addition to a symbolic mode, modern Western experience is characterized by an inner/outer separation of mind and matter, idea and entity, subject and object. For Westerners, what happens in the mind is "subjective," separate from and having no effect upon the "objective" world. This disconnection causes us to view the world in a detached way, as something to be used or something to be preserved. To us, the world does not have psychological life of its own, because psyche or "soul" lies only *within* the individual. In Christianity the kingdom of heaven lies within. In medicine getting to the source means delving within the body, literally, through x-rays, surgery, and injections. In psychotherapy the universe is interiorized; knowing the universe is knowing one's inner life.

In the Navajo world, knowledge, thought, and speech are connected with beauty and have the power to affect the material world. Indeed, the world was created through beauty in thought, language, and speech. The world came into being when the Holy People went into the primal *hogan* or dwelling hut, became aware of the world's forms, organized them through thought, and gave them concrete reality through language.

> The earth will be
> the mountains will be
> (and so on, mentioning other things to be)
> The earth will be, from ancient times
> with me there is knowledge of it.
> The mountains will be, from ancient times
> with me there is knowledge of it.
> The earth will be, from the very beginning
> I have thought it.
> The mountains will be, from the very beginning
> I have thought it.
> The earth will be from ancient times
> I speak it.
> The mountains will be, from ancient times
> I speak it.
>
> (Witherspoon 1977, 16)

For the Navajo, things are because they are first known, then thought, and finally spoken.

The power of language is illustrated in the everyday life of the Navajo through the fear of gossip and witchcraft. The Navajo will never talk about death or accidents for fear the words themselves will bring about the event. There was considerable conflict among the staff of the clinic where I worked when the clinic was required to perform a disaster drill in order to fulfill certification requirements. To the traditional members of the staff, practicing the event in words would have the power to bring about the event. The "damage" caused by the disaster drill could only be undone through the ritual language of a singer who was hired to perform a chant for the clinic.

For the Navajo, the magical power inherent in the word itself has the power of healing: "It commands, compels, organizes, transforms, and restores. It disperses evil, reverses disorder, neutralizes pain, overcomes fear, eliminates illness, relieves anxiety, and restores order, health and well being" (Witherspoon 1977, 34). It is the word itself which has psychological life. The word is the speaker, the mover, the healer.

The Navajo living in beauty will sense the god, the hill, the plant, the animal, and the social community as animated entities with which he strives for proper relationship, relationship reflected in language. In the healing ceremonies, all these entities are invoked in the name of beauty for their healing power. The aesthetic vision is an everyday sensual vision, one that sees the significance of things in their appearance, which is guided according to relationship with appearance, and which grants healing power to appearance. For the Navajo, beauty is a way of everyday life. A Navajo daily prayer, analogous to the Lord's Prayer:

> With beauty before me, I walk
> With beauty behind me, I walk
> With beauty above me, I walk
> With beauty below me, I walk
> From the East beauty has been restored
> From the South beauty has been restored
> From the West beauty has been restored
> From the North beauty has been restored
> From the zenith in the sky beauty has been restored
> From the nadir of the earth beauty has been restored
> From all around me beauty has been restored
> In old age wandering, I walk
> Now on the trail of beauty, I walk.
>
> (Witherspoon 1977, 153–54)

Navajo Aesthetic

The Navajo worldview is based on an aesthetic of interrelatedness and unity. Witherspoon finds four specific elements that contribute to this aesthetic: control, containment, order, and creation. These four elements are all reflected in the daily life and healing of the Navajo.

Control of emotion and behavior brings about harmony in the life of the Navajo. Display or expression of emotion and passionate behavior is shunned. Excess is avoided because it implies lack of control. In doing art therapy with Navajo children, I was particularly impressed by the care and attention that every child gave to any piece of work. The need for control and respect for the line permeate all Navajo craftwork and parallels the sense of control that the surgeon or engineer uses in the West. Psychopathology among the Navajo is directly related to the breakdown of the cultural value placed on control. Kaplan and Johnson (1969) have described three categories through which emotional "dis-ease" is expressed among the

Navajo: "moth craziness" is an epileptic-like condition believed to relate to incest; "ghost sickness" is a disorder related to being witched, carrying symptoms of anxiety, bad dreams, and delirium; "crazy violence" is a condition in which the individual becomes spontaneously and violently out of control, physically assaulting persons and objects in the environment regardless of consequence. The common denominator in all these disorders is a movement toward demonic possession and away from the cultural value of control.

Control also plays an important role in Navajo healing ceremonies in which chants and sandpaintings are performed and crafted to perfection. The chants, consisting of songs and prayers, bring the patient into identification with mythical figures and into right relationship with the gods. These chants, many of which go on all night or extend over several days, must be sung word-perfectly or the ceremony will be useless.

The sandpaintings are mythical designs or images ranging in size from 18 inches to 12 feet in diameter; they are created on the ground of the ceremonial hut or hogan by the singer and his helpers. The designs vary from ceremony to ceremony, and each different part of a single ceremony calls for a particular design. The paintings also must be made to perfection or the ceremony will be of no use or, even worse, will have a malevolent effect on the patient.

A sense of containment permeates Navajo culture. The Reservation itself is contained geographically within four sacred mountains that form its boundaries in each of the four directions. Containment is reflected in the healing rites through the *temenos* or sacred place provided by the ceremonial *hogan* and in the sandpaintings, the ritual containers of the universe.

The Navajo blanket contains the individual within the universal. Contemporary Anglo weaver Jana Vander Lee has pointed out that Navajo blankets were originally woven with horizontal stripes that became vertical when worn over the shoulders. Vander Lee asserts that the vertical line of the blanket reinforces the vertical line of the spinal column, becoming what Eliade refers to as a "cosmic pillar." Vander Lee (unpublished) writes:

> The Navajo blanket became a symbolic link in the relationship of a universal, abstract pattern, symbolizing the cosmos, which was wrapped around a unique, individual person. Wearing the blanket reiterated humanity enveloped by the harmony of nature, as part of a universal pattern. The Indian, in the blanket, united a sense of cosmic and physical order.

Finally, the existence of the Navajo child is contained by cultural forms. The fetus is protected in utero by a complex set of taboos that the pregnant mother must follow. The infant is kept in a cradle board, contained between a wooden back, Mother Earth, and the arch over its head, Father Sky. The child is traditionally given his or her sense of place in relationship to the clan by stories related by grandparents during winter evenings. These stories not only connect the child with the clan but also with the cosmos, for they tell how the clan originated out of mythological times.

Order is a central element in the Navajo aesthetic and a basic theme in its mythology. The original people were led up out of the underworld through ascending levels of order. Heroes overcame chaotic beings not by killing them but by ordering their energy and knowledge. In Navajo tradition, there are extensive and complex ordering systems for clans, taboos, and word usage. Symmetry is a predominant factor in the Navajo sense of order, which parallels the perceived order of nature. Symmetry of gender orders dwellings and ceremonies as well as rainfall into male and female categories.

Order is paramount in the healing process. Sandpaintings and chants are designed and structured in symmetrical patterns. Chants often depict a perfectly orchestrated movement out of the ceremonial hut into the world, a confrontation with a divinity, and finally a return to the hut. During the all-night singing of the Nine Night Chant, after the songs depicting the journey of the patient's spirit have been sung, the singer sings the "Song of the Blue Bird." It is sung at exactly that time before dawn when the blue birds actually are awakening and singing to each other outside the ceremonial hut.

The act of creation or making is integral to the Navajo way of life; one experiences beauty by creating it. Mythologically, the primordial aesthetic act was the creation of the universe when the holy people went into the primal hut and sang the world into being. Traditionally, every Navajo is well versed in a craft—weaving, leather work, basketry, or silversmithing.

Songs play an especially important part in Navajo life. The songs sung every day maintain the individual in *ho'zho'*. Every traditional Navajo knows or "possesses" songs of many different types. One's wealth is not measured in terms of money but in terms of one's songs. There are riding songs, walking songs, grinding songs, planting songs, growing songs, and harvesting songs. There are songs to greet the sun in the morning and songs to bid it farewell in the evening. There are songs for horses, songs for sheep, songs for blessing a *hogan,* and songs for taking a sweat bath. The most powerful songs are the ritual songs used in the healing ceremonies or "sings" by Navajo healers known as "singers." The songs sung every day maintain the individual in *ho'zho'*.

The most dramatic creations of the Navajo are the sandpaintings made for the curing ceremonies. Each painting is made by the singer and his helpers on the day that it is to be used, and must be created in all of its intricate workings without a flaw. The design of the painting is a reproduction of the design acquired by the mythical hero from the god or demonic adversary. The patient sits on the sandpainting, and in doing so is brought into direct identification with the healing powers of the gods. The image itself heals. The singer helps in the process of identification by alternately touching various parts of the body of the god in the painting and the corresponding parts of the patient's body.

Every ceremony is a grand creation on a cosmic scale, a re-creation of the universe on three different levels. The gathering of singers in the ceremonial hut replicates the gathering of holy people in the primordial hut to sing the universe into being. The content of the chants takes the patient back into primordial times when the universe came into being. The making of the sandpainting itself reflects the making of the universe.

We can see that in the Navajo world beauty heals through cultural forms. "Beauty way" is brought into being through aesthetic qualities of order, control, containment, and creative action—all overt cultural modes of aligning the psyche with forms that transcend the individual. Order manifests in the symmetry of the chant motifs and sandpainting designs. Containment lies in the sacred space of the ceremonial hut and in the sandpainting designs. Control reveals itself in the perfection and precision with which the ceremony is performed. Creation emerges in the singing of the chants and the making of the sandpaintings, reenactments of the creation of the universe.

To paraphrase a former Indian Health Service psychiatrist, Robert Bergman, Navajo ceremonials could be likened to a Western spectacle in which a lecture, psychoanalysis, High Mass, grand opera, major surgery, and the unveiling of a masterpiece are all going on at once. In the Navajo world, art is not imprisoned in museums, performance not confined to theaters, healing not closeted in hospitals and therapy chambers, intellectual life not relegated to academia, and religion not compartmentalized into churches. For the Navajo, the lecture is the performance, the prayer is the operation, the painting and the song are the cure. Art, religion, biology, medicine, epistemology, and ontology are all one. Beauty is being.

We look to the Navajo for spiritual guidance, but the Navajo direct us back to the forms inherent in our own cultural vision. The Navajo sense of language points us back to the life of language in the Western tradition. The ancient Greeks saw language itself as having curative power, a notion that was reborn in the "talking cure" of psychoanalysis. In the analytic situation both therapist and patient become witness to the "story" that is created (Hillman 1983). Through language, the life wanderings, the necessary tribulations, the particular pattern of follies, entanglements, and confused identities all unfold, becoming the particular myth of the patient.

As we will see in the next chapter, the Navajo sense of image directs us back to the Western tradition of appearance itself as the holder of meaning. For example, Plotinus, the philosopher of love and beauty, wrote that all forming, all creating, all action is inherent in vision itself. Both the Navajo and Plotinus teach us that the ability to organize experience through the perception of larger forms, seeing through imagination, is at once the acting, the knowing, and the being.

The Navajo is a culture in which forms that transcend the individual, what we might experience as "death," are acknowledged and honored. In subsequent chapters we explore several forms that encompass our daily Western experience, covertly in-forming us through the mysteries of death.

A New Culture

As Western ways permeate the traditional Navajo culture in most areas of the Reservation, it finds itself fast fragmenting, its center breaking apart losing its hold on the people. Now it is not Kit Carson but video game figures who invade even the most remote trading posts, cutting off heads. The discussion at gatherings of singers soon turns into a litany of despair over their dying world. The old stories are no longer generally told to children; taboos are broken. Knowledge of and respect for sacred places are wavering among the people. Ever since President Johnson's "War on Poverty," the medium of exchange has become money instead of goods to trade, and with the crumbling of the old economic system, the identity of the people is disappearing as well. As the Navajo world becomes anglicized, experience becomes interiorized, the universe falls within the individual personality; myth and ritual drop into the "unconscious."

An anglicized Navajo woman whom I supervised described her experience of traveling off the Reservation for the first time by herself to attend social work school in southern Arizona. After leaving the Reservation and driving south, she had to stop her car along the side of the road while she cried in grief over leaving her home. That night she had a dream of coming to a river and trying to find a way across. Later, I came upon a Navajo chant through which I realized that myth, having lost its cultural support, was making itself known through the unconscious of this individual's psyche just as in the Western world. This woman truly was experiencing a mythological event. In the chant the hero of the ceremonial, Mountaintop Way, crosses southward into unknown territory, leaving his homeland behind him to the north. He looks to his homeland and a feeling of loneliness and homesickness sweeps over him. He weeps and sings.

> That flowing water! That flowing water!
> My mind wanders across it.
> That broad water! That broad water!
> My mind wanders across it.
> That old age water! That flowing water!
> My mind wanders across it.

As the Navajo world breaks down in many areas of the Reservation, so also do its healing practices. Navajo singers become fewer in number, and many ceremonies have already died out. There is drunkenness at ceremonies (even among singers), families can no longer be counted on to participate as a unit in the preparations. Many patients have lost their connection with the traditional Navajo world, and with it, they have lost their underlying faith in its healing practices.

A third worldview is emerging, however, from the present interface of the two conflicting cultures—something similar to the relatively new religion of the Native American Church. As this happens, so also will a new form of healing evolve that will reflect psyche as it is manifested in the new world of Westernized Navajo.

Now the vision fades and memory wanes as the old men of the desert gather, two or three at a time, on the occasion of dis-ease and dis-order, to repeat together the primordial creation of the universe, to paint the old pictures, to tell the old tales, to sing the old songs, to chant the cosmos into renewed being yet one more time. They see only feelingly now, as they make their way—

"Is it turquoise here?"

"No, the abalone."

"The yellow corn there?"

"Yes, and then the white . . ."

". . . then Corn Girl and Blue Bird . . ."

". . . and then Dawn Boy . . ."

as they make their way, one last time, through the long Navajo night.

CHAPTER TWO

Beauty as Appearance

Beauty works actively on the perceptible. Beauty gives relief to the contemplated world and is an elevation in the dignity of seeing at the same time. (Bachelard 1971, 185)

The world men are born into contains many things, natural and artificial, living and dead, transient and sempiternal, all of which have in common that they *appear* and hence are meant to be seen, heard, touched, tasted and smelled, to be perceived by sentient creatures. . . . In this world which we enter, appearing from a nowhere and from which we disappear into a nowhere, *Being and Appearing coincide*. (Arendt 1977, 19)

To speak of our everyday experience as the perception of appearance is to speak in the language of aesthetics; it is to speak of beauty. I would like to talk about the subject of beauty as a way of approaching one of the major themes in this book: how appearance is the ground of everyday life. My purpose in this chapter is twofold: (1) to recover a true sensibility, essence, or soul of beauty that has been lost in modern life, and (2) to see how beauty is a matter of soul or essence in our lives.

What Is Beauty?

In addressing beauty, the first thing we encounter is resistance. To speak of beauty is embarrassing. We usually think of beauty as something inferior— effete as opposed to substantial, soft as juxtaposed to hard facts, passive instead of active, ornate and decorative as compared to foundational, an attribute of something else rather than valued in and of itself. We think of beauty as relative ("beauty lies in the eye of the beholder"), and therefore somehow unreal because not objective.[1] Beauty is superficial; "you can't tell a book by looking at its cover," or beauty is only "skin deep," as opposed to something essential.

Beauty can't be fixed nor does it serve our need for control. We literalize beauty and separate it off from the mainstream of our everyday lives. We segregate beauty into museums, galleries, studios, and theaters, as belonging to a segment of life we call "art," or we preserve it in areas away from everyday life which we designate as "nature." As a correlate of our sense of beauty as something subjective and separate from everyday life, we designate people as artists or critics who have special talents and sensibilities who are qualified to talk about, know, or create beauty. We then idealize beauty by paying inflated prices in the purchase of objects of art or theater tickets. At the other extreme, when budgets are crunched, the category for aesthetic values is the first to go, the farthest from the "bottom line" of economic consideration.[2]

Our resistance to beauty has its background in the Hebrew, Platonic, Stoic, and Christian traditions. The Hebrew god, Yahweh, insisted upon faith in His invisible spiritual presence so that the worship of image was sinful. In the Platonic tradition, truth lies in the invisibility and fixity of the infinite forms that cannot be apprehended by the mortal soul. What the mortal perceives are only replicas, appearance being the mere imitation or signification of the divine.

Stoics experienced earthly life as oppressive and emphasized strength of will in the service of freeing consciousness from the suffering and necessities of the world. Will was strengthened by the turn of consciousness from external life toward an introverted quest for the invisibilities of spirit. Paraphrasing Epictetus, Arendt writes:

> The power of the will rests on its sovereign decision to concern itself only with things within man's power, and these reside exclusively in human inwardness. . . . Everything that seems to be real, the world of appearance, actually needs my consent in order to be real for me. And this consent cannot be forced on me: if I withhold it, then the reality of the world disappears as though it were a mere apparition. (Arendt 1978, 78)

With the advent of Christianity,

> the accent shifts entirely from doing to believing, from the outward man living in a world of appearances (himself an appearance

among appearances and therefore subject to semblance and illusion) to an inwardness which by definition never unequivocally manifests itself and can be scrutinized only by a God who also never appears unequivocally. (Arendt 1977, 67)[3]

In sum, the diminution of appearance in the service of spirit held the advantage of enhancing individual will.

The Reformation continued the Church's rejection of image in favor of a purely spiritual orientation based solely on faith. Milton demonstrates the Protestant emphasis on the inferiority of form and imagination by locating these qualities in "woman." The characters of Delilah and Eve are subordinate counterparts to the males, Samson and Adam, who are connected to God through reason. Eve, the embodiment of "sensual appetite," through imagination and sensuous life, is responsible for the Fall.

> For Understanding rul'd not, and the Will
> Heard not her lore, both in subjection now
> To sensual Appetite, who from beneath
> Usurping over sovran Reason claim'd
> Superior sway.
> (*Paradise Lost* IX 1127–31)

In the Western tradition, the movement of consciousness to inner life eventually became the subjectivity of modernity, a consciousness that locates the source of all life in the interiority of the mind. As a result, the mathematical tools of science were required to apprehend the truth of the world. Beauty, as the appearance of form, became subjected to reason and interiority as derivatives of spirit. The truth of things became not how they appeared or were experienced, but the mathematical qualities derived from concepts applied to them.

The Homeric Greeks had an alternative idea of beauty and the aesthetic essence of things. In this tradition, beauty was a force in the world that allowed for the appearance and being of things, events and consciousness itself. Beauty was not "in the eye of the beholder," but the medium through which one perceived and existed. This force was personified in the goddess, Aphrodite, the essence of beauty. Aphrodite represented divinity accessible to mortals because she, alone among the divinities, revealed herself to humans as bodily being.

Aphrodite's beauty came not from adherence to a norm, but through unselfconscious, radiant presence. The Greeks called this force *kalos,* from which we get our word "quality." It is related to the Greek word *kalleo,* to call or provoke, *kalos* being that which calls us into the world. *Kalos* was associated with self-presentation, that which could be seen, as opposed to that which was known through invisible, abstract concept or principle. The Greek word *aisthesis,* from which we get our term "aesthetic," means "manifest to sense." The senses, instead of being suspicious or misleading, were the basis of perceiving the truth of things.

Kalos pertained to people and things, to gods, and to the actions of both gods and humans. Through *kalos,* parts, fragments, and details could be seen as wholes in themselves, because each part had its own perfection. *Kalos* was related to fine shape, fairness in form, nobility in bearing, and the auspicious. It had to do with right action, sacrifice, honesty, nobility, justice, and the straightforward. Something existed in *kalos* to the extent that it could be valued in and of itself, not because it was useful in the service of something else or was a means to a larger end. Kenneth Clark says of Botticelli's painting of Aphrodite, "her face reveals no thought beyond the present" (Clark 1956, 101). In other words, the beauty of Aphrodite makes any movement to "meaning," as derived from an abstract system or an authority beyond what appears in the moment, unnecessary. From this position, what we call "truth" lies in the presenting form, the appearance, the body of experience itself.

Aphrodite was called the "shining one" and her beauty lay in a radiance that was central to her nature. Plato said that Beauty alone, of all the infinite Forms, was intelligible to humans. The Greeks called this intelligibility *ekphanestaton,* "showing itself." Beauty in the Aphrodisian mode is a matter of appearance or display, shining forth (in German the word for appearance is *Ersheinung*). Something is beautiful to the extent that it shines forth in the luster of its own particularity or peculiarity or individuality, and in this display, its meaning is revealed. When I am "red" with anger, the redness doesn't have to be interpreted to represent anger. It *is* the anger itself showing forth. The word "phenomenon," indicating what we think of as a "happening," has its root in the Greek *phos,* which means "light." From this perspective, what we call "experience" would be the spark of divinity that reveals itself in everyday form through the power of light or beauty. Beauty, as a matter of light, is the force that allows for the perception of things and experience of events in the displays, exhibitions, and presentations of everyday life. Beauty is what brings our lives together and makes them tangible.

The ancient idea of beauty provides us with several implications that give a depth to experience. Beauty is a way of understanding through imagination. Our bias is that imagination is unreal, and we attribute reality to what is literal. For the Greeks, appearance (*eidos*) occurred through *phainesthati* or imagination. Perception, here, is prior to an inner/outer distinction. When imagination is seen as the basis of all perception, as beauty itself, everything has its own truth. The power of beauty brings a truth to every moment and event, to all of experience. At the same time, spirit and matter, energy and form are congealed into a living form, a bodily being. Here, every moment becomes religious in the sense that beauty is the "Redeemer," the power that brings out the perfection in each thing, event, person, or moment. The divine is close at hand in ordinary, "profane" situations, but it takes the imaginative eye to perceive it. Modern artists help us by seeing that beauty lies in the mundane soup can, a pile of junk, a stream of urine, or the wreckage of an accident. It isn't just the norm or symmetrical that is valid, truthful, or beautiful, rather, even the grotesque can have its own beauty.

For William Blake, the power of imagination was personified in Los, the archetypal craftsman and artist. Los's halls are filled with every conscious moment that ever took place, each moment depicted as a work of art.

> All things acted on Earth are seen in the bright Sculptures of
> Los's Halls & every Age renews its powers from these Works
> With every pathetic story possible to happen from Hate or
> Wayward Love & every sorrow & distress is carved here
> Every Affinity of Parents Marriages & Friendships are here
> In all their various contaminations wrought with wondrous Art
> All that can happen to Man in his pilgrimage.
>
> (*Jerusalem* I, 61–67)

In contrast, we usually value the big picture over the particular thing or event, the map over the place itself. We see beauty in symmetry, proportion, wholeness, the universal. We consider truth as lying in norms rather than in the particular display of the moment. We attribute validity to tests, statistics, typologies, categories, and systems of interpretation rather than perception of the unique or concrete (Hillman 1980). Blake is showing us that beauty allows for validity in the particularity of individual things and events.

Here, a shadow creeps in. If everything has the potential for beauty, what would be the ugly? Does nothing need to be changed, fixed, or healed? Plato said the ugly was that which was at odds with the divine (*Symposium* 206d). For Plotinus, the ugly was a giving over to that which was of "another order" (*En.* V.8.13). The Renaissance philosopher, Ficino, said the ugly was that which is distant from the First Beauty, or that which is out of relationship with its archetypal form. In other words, something is ugly to the extent that it is out of relationship with its own essence.

To be out of relationship with essence is what Jung referred to as "inauthentic suffering," "neurosis," or "unconsciousness." Our word for that which makes us literally unconscious is "anaesthesia," or not perceptible. "Ugliness" as suffering or pain that comes from inauthentic being is a matter of not being perceptible, and calls for an active adjustment. As we saw in the previous chapter, the Navajo Native Americans treat illness aesthetically by putting the patient into alignment with the appropriate divine form.

Beauty is distinct from the ugly, but it does have its own darkness and frightfulness. Plotinus said, "We are stricken by a salutary terror in the sight of beauty" (*En.* I.6.7). Rilke wrote, "Beauty is the beginning of Terror we're still just able to bear" ("First Elegy"). Wallace Stevens declared, "Death is the mother of beauty," and Yeats referred to "a terrible beauty." Aphrodite was called the "black one," "Aphrodite of the Grave," and "the Dark One." She was born from a severed genital, bore Terror and Fear, was married to the ugly and crippled god, Hephaistos, slept with the god of rage, Ares, and wrecked terrible vengeance on those who betrayed her. Claire Lejeune writes:

> This Beauty is sovereign, because it is unforeseeable and inescapable. Against its possible victory, our defeat, we arm ourselves; we turn from terror to terrorism. The ultimate object of human fear is Beauty; nothing is more disarming, more ravishing, than its eruption in our lives. Beauty alone brings us to our knees without abasement, washes away all humiliation, heals us of all rancor, and reconciles us with the universe. (Paris 1986, 17)

The focus of this book is the darker aspect of beauty, the sense of death that characterizes our experience as created not completely by our wills, but in part by larger forms.

Beauty as Action

While we usually think of beauty in association with a passive stance, the sense that beauty is a force that allows for perception gives it an active quality. *Aisthesis* was originally associated with "breathing in," and *kalos* was associated with "right action." For Plato, the soul in love with beauty moves with great passion toward it, as if on wings or pulled by chariot horses. Perception is not a passive registering of facts, as we usually think of it, but an imaginative "making" or "creation" or "procreation" of a new moment. Creative action is not something that is confined to artists, but a matter of everyday consciousness.

The aesthetic vision entails joining two worlds, that of the seer and that of the seen, producing a third world of "image." Consciousness itself is then a creative act of imagination. Following Jung, we create reality every day through fantasy. Plato described the capacity to formulate in the figures of carpenters and weavers. William Blake portrayed imagination in the persons of Los, a blacksmith, and Enitharmon, a weaver, both engaged in a powerfully active mode of being—the creation of everyday moments. Hillman explains:

> Fantasy-images are both the raw materials and finished products of psyche, and they are the privileged mode of access to knowledge of soul. Nothing is more primary. Every notion in our minds, each perception of the world and sensation in ourselves must go through a psychic organization in order to happen at all. Every single feeling or observation occurs as a psychic event by first forming a fantasy-image. (Hillman 1975c, xi)

When consciousness itself is understood as action, perception itself can be understood as a "gathering" of a world. Martin Heidegger depicts the creation of world as image in his description of Van Gogh's painting of a pair of old peasant shoes.

> From the dark opening of the worn insides of the shoes the toilsome tread of the worker stares forth. In the stiffly rugged heaviness of the shoes there is the accumulated tenacity of her slow trudge through the far-spreading and ever-uniform furrows of the field swept by a raw wind. On the leather lie the dampness and richness of the soil. Under the soles slide the loneliness of the field-path as evening falls. In the shoes vibrates the silent call of the earth, its quiet gift of the ripening grain and its unexplained self-refusal in the fallow desolation of the wintry field. This equipment is pervaded by uncomplaining anxiety as to the certainty of bread, the wordless joy of having once more withstood want, the trembling before the impending childbed and shivering at the surrounding menace of death. This equipment belongs to

the *earth,* and it is protected in the world of the peasant woman. (Heidegger 1971, 34–35)

Beauty as Knowledge

For us, knowing is a matter of control; we control something in order to know it. We take data derived from the scientific method as knowledge, and the scientific method is based on controlling situations in which data is accumulated in order to reduce variables. In antiquity, to theorize meant to reflect upon that which was beyond human understanding, as opposed to praxis, that which could be made by mortal hands. We have lost the sense of understanding as "standing under," that is, deriving truth through contemplation of the appearance of a thing or event itself. Instead, we "stand over" experience with our systems, tests, and instruments of measurement, mistrustful of our own experience.

For the Greeks, knowledge was a matter of the sensual. One knows through seeing and what one sees, one knows. The Greek word for perception is *aisthesis,* meaning "of the senses," the verb *aisthanomai* means both "to sense" and "to know." The Greek word for "form" was *eidos,* that which is perceived, while the verb *eidenai* means "to see" but also "to know." Truth was *alethia,* that which was revealed through a "shining forth" of light. For Plato, knowing was a matter of gathering up perceptions so that they made a form; the soul was attracted to the world, because the world's forms reminded the soul of the eternal Forms it once knew. Knowing was a matter of remembering.

In Plato's imagination, the soul on its way to knowledge was first attracted by the human body. So knowing through beauty is a sensual, bodily knowing—not knowing through the detached vision of the objective eye. With erotic seeing, no journey of interpretation is needed; image and meaning are one. The French phenomenologist, Maurice Merleau-Ponty, wrote: "To see is to enter a universe of beings which *display themselves . . .* to look at an object is to inhabit it and from this habitation to grasp all things in terms of the aspect which they present to it" (Merleau-Ponty 1962, 68). Jung: "We may say that the image represents the meaning of the instinct" (Jung 1960, 201). "Image and meaning are identical and as the first takes shape, so the latter becomes clear. Actually the pattern needs no interpretation, it portrays its own meaning" (Jung 1960, 204).

The idea that is presenting itself is that we are always living within a particular understanding, a particular form. To see imaginatively is to see that perception is the creation of a world or, using William Blake's words, there is "a world in a grain of sand" ("Auguries of Innocence") if we can just see it. Every perception is a co-creation of a new world. Heidegger called this "worlding," and Blake described the worlding of every moment of consciousness as

> an immortal Tent built by the Sons of Los,
> And every Space that a Man views around his dwelling-place,
> Standing on his own roof, or in his garden on a mount
> Of twenty-five cubits in height, such space is his Universe;
> And on its verge the sun rises and sets, the Clouds bow
> To meet the flat earth & the Sea in such an order'd Space,
> The Starry heavens reach no further, but here bend and set
> On all sides, & the two Poles turn on their valves of gold.
> And if he move his dwelling-place, his heavens also move
> Where'er he goes, & all his neighbourhood bewail his loss.
> Such are the Spaces called Earth & such its dimension.
>
> (*Milton*, plate 28)

Beauty as Being

When beauty is a force in the world, self-presentation or appearance is a value in and of itself. Aphrodite is the goddess of cosmetics, and the word *cosmos* means "the right placing of things." So when we make up the face in the morning, we are at the same time honoring the cosmic face of things. The Swiss biologist Adolph Portman (1967) suggests there is in nature an innate urge for display that cannot be explained by the theory of evolution or survival of the species. In other words, plants and animals appear in an incredible variety and complexity of forms, not so that they can survive, but from a natural instinct for display. Nature wants to be seen. Concepts like natural selection, sexual attraction, and camouflage do not explain the complexity or variety or colors of patterns in the coats, wings, and horns of animals and leaves of plants. Portman gives as evidence the beautiful forms and colors of fish that exist in the deepest, darkest part of the sea where there is no chance that their survival depends on the attraction of their appearance because there is no light to see it. The peacock's multicolored tail is not the most attracting aspect of its mating presentation. Mollusk shells with their beautiful shapes and curves are at the bottom of the evolutionary ladder.

The event of seeing and being seen, then, has its own inherent value. Alphonso Lingis writes:

> Glory is for its witness, the spectacle is for the spectator, the screen of phenomenal effects produced in reality are for a sphere of lucidity, an eye, a mind! With this inference one makes even the gloss of appearance intelligible, and one posits oneself as an essential and necessary factor in the sphere which one enters. One appropriates even this film of semblance and this vanity of appearances. *Omnia ad maiorem gloriam deo*—God himself was said to have been obliged to create man to receive the splendor of his glory. (Lingis 1983, 9)

In some graffiti, Blake wrote, "imagination is not a state, it is existence." We live *in* image, or as Jung said, "images are life" (Jung 1970, 180). When we live in image, we live in metaphor. The roots of the definition of the word "metaphor" refer to carrying something from one place to another, the creation of connection between two worlds. While we think we are in a certain condition, or headed in a particular direction, or working upon something, something else is happening, something is working upon or feeling or speaking or writing or playing through us. When we are depressed or angry or frustrated or fearful or lonely, something else is happening as well, something is being created out of the heat of our anger and the grinding of our frustrations or washed away by the tears of our sadnesses.

In our age of analytical science, psychological awareness, and psychotherapy, we think we can know ourselves and our world from a position of control. Beauty would teach us otherwise. If we exist in a particular mode or form of understanding, then we can never really "know" anything except through that larger form. Thus, consciousness is always flitting back and forth in a kind of play between "truth" and "meaning." We think we have it, an idea, a feeling, a perception, an attitude, but it also has us. Beauty is what allows the form to intimate itself to us, but the experience is not comfortable. It takes us out of the certainty we have when we ascribe the life of the soul to something outside ourselves. Beauty teaches us we are always in and out of the night sea, forever in and out of the belly of the whale on the journey toward meaning, perpetually existing dimly in and out of awareness.

In these first two chapters, I have been establishing the idea of a larger-than-life aspect of our existence. It is accessible through imagination and has the effect of a kind of death. The "something larger than us," the other, lies in the stuff of our experience and is wanting to be recognized. It is already working on us, changing us. This "other" that encompasses us has many forms,[4] and ensuing chapters explore some of the manifestations of these forms in everyday life—play, technology, relationship, violence, race—through which death makes itself known.

PART TWO

Death as Invisible

CHAPTER THREE

Ball/Play

The Soul of Game

There we would stand
within the gap left between world and toy
upon a spot which, from the first beginning
had been established for a pure event.
—Rainer Marie Rilke

All this, when will all this have been . . . just play?
—Samuel Beckett

As a boy growing up in the Midwest, I would go with my family to church on Sunday mornings. When the minister was preaching I would invariably find myself entertaining unruly feelings and fantasies of all sorts, one of which concerned a ball. In my imagination I would toss the ball to the preacher, and he would throw it back. I would lob it up to the choir in the loft, and the choir members would flip it around and then back to me. I would bounce it off the wall and then up to the parishioners in the balcony. The ball would continue around the sanctuary, soaring and falling, rebounding or going directly to various individuals. It was as if the ball itself "served" to take me out of my subjective consciousness, to gather the community, and to create a religious event.

Conversely, I had an immediate religious experience whenever I entered a gymnasium or a ball field; I would feel becalmed or "held" as if entering a holy place. The smell of the waxed gymnasium floor on a cold winter night or the dewy grass of the playing field on an autumn evening drew me into their space. The geometrical shapes formed by the painted or limed boundary

---

This chapter is dedicated to Coach Burt Hable of West High School, Madison, Wisconsin, who taught his players the deeper value of playing with passion and precision for the sake of the game itself.

lines contained me. Self-consciousness would fall away, body and mind would unite, and play would take over with a life of its own.

I identified with the heroic aspect of the ball player, warrior fighting the enemy, and played in different sports for several years. Finally, I reached my level of incompetence in four traumatically unsuccessful years of football at a major college. At this point my interests turned elsewhere, and the "ball player" receded into the shadowy spaces of my psyche.

Subsequently, I started having dreams that continued for several years, dreams of returning to the teams and coaches, the games and practices, with which I had been associated previously. The dreams had several recurring themes representing different forms of anxiety—being in various positions of unpreparedness for play, making the wrong play, coming from behind with time running out, enduring the wrath or contempt of my college football coach. In one sense, my career as an athlete was being revealed by my dreams as an initiation gone wrong, a failed attempt at coming into my own as an adult male through successful combat.

The dreams were like the recurring traumatic dreams of Vietnam war veterans that indicated the failure of that war as an initiation of U.S. soldiers into manhood (Wilmer 1986). The repetitive nature of the dreams was an indication of my psyche's attempt to work through the trauma. For example, a transformation in my usual identity as a benchwarming outcast and my usual ("right-handed") mode of "going by the book" or retreating into study was revealed in the following dream:

> College football game. As usual, I am late, can't find all the parts of my uniform, especially helmet and spikes, and I know the coach is angry at me. I grab some books to read on the bench and run out onto the field to join my teammates who are already in the heat of the game. Inexplicably, I wander into the end zone toward which my team is heading. My team has the ball at the opposite end of the field and is heading in my direction. A black, left-handed quarterback on our team by the name of "Farr" throws a pass the entire length of the field into the end zone where I am standing. I am the only one near where the ball is coming down, it is coming right for me and there is nothing to do but try to catch it. In order to catch the ball, I have to use my left hand because my right is holding books. I catch the ball with my left hand scoring a touchdown. For the rest of the game I feel accepted by the coach and players as part of the team.

In another series of dreams, a change in the critical, hostile authority in my psyche, which we usually associate with father, was revealed in changes that occurred in my college coach. In one dream, he kept a secret garden on the roof over the locker room, in another he had children and a family, in another he wept, and in one he was glad to see me in a place outside the playing area where we could have a conversation.

The following dream revealed a focus on a new, hidden element that was "driving" me that had to do with what Jung called "anima" or femininity, lightness of foot, dancing, and sensitivity emerging in the midst of an aggressive, goal-directed, authoritarian world.

> I am driving a truck to the team meeting to deliver the film of the team's practice to be viewed by the coaches and players. I am wearing a ballet slipper on my right foot which I have on the gas petal. I am glad that no one can see this slipper. I deliver the film, and it is projected on the screen for all to see. It turns out that the entire length of film is a shot of my foot in a ballet slipper! Apparently the camera, which had been at my side on the seat of the truck, had been rolling all the time while aimed at my foot. I am very embarrassed.

In another instance, the difficulty I was having in integrating the "ball player" of my psyche was depicted by a dream as a split between an ego ideal, what I thought I wanted to be, and the ball player of whom I was ashamed.

> I am at a college at a lecture being given by a famous lecturer. A black man who washes dishes and plays football is in the audience. Throughout the lecture, the lecturer complains about the football player being there, and at one point tries to throw him out physically, chasing him around the auditorium, and even up a rope hanging on stage. The students are cheering for the black man.

Finally, a change in my propensity for sabotaging myself was displayed in the following dream:

> I am sitting in the stands watching a football game. One team is punting toward their opponent's goal line. The punt looks like a perfect "coffin corner" kick, giving the opposing team no space from which to run its plays. I am the only one in the stadium to see that the ball actually missed the "coffin corner" by a fraction

of an inch, and the opposing team should get the ball out on the twenty-yard line with plenty of room to run its plays.

This dream indicates not only how good I was at "punting" in life and putting myself in the "coffin corner" with no room to operate, but that I now had perspective to see that there was a chance to give myself some room to run.

Years later, I came across two short passages in the work of Jung where he mentions a ball game played by priests as part of a *festum fatuorum* (1954, 258) and ritual ball games played in churches (McGuire 1984, 25). In reading the notes, I remembered my fantasies as a boy in church, and started thinking about the ball game and my experience as a ball player in terms of religious events. My renewed thinking eventually took me to the ancient Mayan ball game, associated sacrificial rituals, and the philosophy of play.

In this chapter I explore the underlying religious elements in the ball game, focusing on the Mayan creation myth, the ancient Mayan ball game, and the ritual of sacrificial beheading that accompanied the game. Finally, these events will be seen as metaphors for everyday life as a form of play in the service of death.

Myth

> We are merely the stars' tennis balls, struck and bandied
> which way please them.
>
> —John Webster

The classic Mayans were a highly evolved culture. They had an astute sense of time and a remarkably precise and complicated calendar. Their architecture was intricately related to the movement of astronomical bodies, and their social system was highly complex. For the Mayans, the ball game was the core of their religious life. Their arch heroes were ball players, and the ball game lay at the heart of their central myth, the *Popol Vuh* (Tedlock 1985).

> Two brothers, One and Seven Hunapuh, are playing ball one day with the sons of One Hunapuh at a location called the "Great Abyss" on the road to the underworld, Xibalba, "place of fright." The lords of Xibalba are offended by the noise of the ball play and lack of deference to themselves. In addition they become desirous of the equipment used by the ball players. The lords issue a challenge to the brothers to bring their equipment and ball to the underworld to play with them. One and Seven Hunapuh take up the

challenge and depart for the underworld. They leave their equipment behind, however, under the roof of their mother's house.

We can see that ball play is located in association with the underworld, an abysmal and frightful realm. Apparently, the underworld gods have a connection with the ball game; ball play stirs them, and the gods have needs that ball players can satisfy. The brothers leave their equipment behind under the roof of their mother. The sexual symbolism here indicates that although the boys leave their mother physically, they are still under her domination psychologically. In an archetypal sense, they are still sons of the Great Mother (Bly 1990).

One and Seven Hunapuh start on their journey. After overcoming several impediments, they enter the underworld where they succumb to practical jokes set up by the lords of the underworld. They mistake two manikins for gods and burn themselves on the bench of hot rocks provided for them. The lords are greatly amused.

The first "road trip" is under way, and the first instance of "benchwarming" takes place. Play extends to and connects with the underworld, and entrance to the underworld involves play. Practical jokes are an initiation into the underworld, just as Freud (1963) has shown that jokes are an initiation into unconscious life.

The brothers are to spend the night in the Dark House, but they fail in keeping their lights going all night. The next day they are sacrificed for this failure and are buried at the Place of the Ballgame Sacrifice. The head of One Hunapuh is placed in a calabash tree.

The ball game has something to do with death. In fact, the Mayan word for ball court, *hom,* is the same as the word for graveyard. Play is for keeps, and the endgame we call "sudden death" can happen at any time.

Blood Woman, daughter of an Xibalban lord, goes to the calabash tree at the Place of the Ballgame Sacrifice and engages in conversation with the head of One Hunapuh. The head spits in her hand, magically impregnating her. Upon hearing the news of her pregnancy, her outraged father orders her to be sacrificed. She tricks him and flees to the Middleworld where she bears the hero twins, Hunapuh and Xbalanque.

The severed head, which will come to be associated with the ball itself, has a life of its own. It talks, spits, and engenders. For the Greeks, the head was the seat of the soul (Onians 1951, 95ff.). Jung speaks of the ancient tradition of the "mysterious head," for example, that of Osiris, and the "oracular head," such as that of Orpheus (1969, 239ff.). In alchemy, the severed head was the *caput corvi,* the head of the raven signifying the state of *nigredo*—depression, putrification, and death (Jung 1970, 510). The alchemists also thought of the head as the *vas,* the container for the soul (Jung 1968c, 87, 267, 433n; 1967, 86). Many myths depict rolling heads chasing after heroes or heroines before taking their place in the sky as heavenly bodies (Gillespie 1991, 325–30). The severed head, then, is a numinous image with supernatural powers and is associated with soul.

> Hunapuh and Xbalanque grow and undergo many adventures as hero twins. They try their hand at farming, but fail. A rat explains why: as the sons of a ball player, they are not destined to be farmers, but ball players. The equipment of their father is waiting for them, hanging under the roof of their grandmother's house. The boys trick grandmother into leaving the house, the rat chews through the rope holding their equipment, and it falls into their hands. The boys sweep out the old court of their father, don their equipment and become the ball players they were meant to be.

"Ball player" is revealed here as a category of identity, a mode, model, or form into which an individual personality can fit: not farmer, but ball player. With mythic god-heroes as ball players, kings and urchin boys alike can identify with the divine through ball playing. The ball and equipment dropping into play is the prototype for the theme of "fall" into play (enacted in the jump ball, flip of the coin, scrum, etc.), which will be repeated in the boys' next movement down into the underworld and in the sacrificial ritual of rolling the victim down a stairway to his death.

> Once again the lords of the underworld are disturbed by ball play above in the Middleworld. Once again they send a message to the offending players, offering a challenge and directing them to bring their equipment. And once again, the challenge is accepted. Hunapuh and Xbalanque travel to Xibalba with their equipment. Like their father before them, they overcome the traps set up for them by the lords, but unlike their father, they are not taken in by the lords' practical jokes. They survive the first night in the Dark

House, setting up the game for the next day. After an argument between the brothers and the gods over whose ball will be used, the lords' will prevails, and their ball is put into play. In fact it is a skull. After it is served by the lords, Hunapuh hits it back. It turns into a flying dagger which twists about in the air, attempting to kill the brothers.

The argument between the boys and the gods is the prototypical opening ritual of playground argument over whose ball will be used. The fact that the skull is a ball gives us our first indication of the association of head and ball. We now have the symbolic configuration ball-head-soul for which death serves as a background. This will be the primary image of the ball game myth/ritual.

The boys protest over the use of a ball which is meant to kill them and threaten to leave. The lords persuade them to stay by allowing the use of their own rubber ball as the game ball. The prize for the first game is to be flowers. The brothers intentionally lose this game and then survive the night in the Razor House. With the help of ants, who have stolen flowers from the lords' garden, the boys give the lords their own flowers the next day (the first Rose Bowl parade?), in effect claiming victory over the gods by having made fools of them.

In succeeding days, games between the boys and the lords of the underworld end in ties, and the boys survive the nights in various houses of death—Cold House, Jaguar House, and Midst of Fire. However, in Bat House, Hunapuh inadvertently loses his head to the sharp wing of a bat and it rolls onto the court. Xbalanque replaces Hunapuh's head with a squash carved like a head, and Hunapuh and Xbalanque make a game plan (the first huddle). The game is played with Hunapuh's head as the ball. Xbalanque hits it out of the court and into a grove of oak trees. The lords chase after the head, but a rabbit acts as a decoy by bouncing along as if it were the ball. Xbalanaque retrieves Hunapuh's actual head, puts it back on him in place of the carved squash and pretends to find the ball which is now the squash. When the lords hit the squash, it splatters, and they are again revealed as fools.

This section of the myth firmly establishes the connection between the ball and severed head. The severed head is soul with autonomous life that becomes the "live" ball as represented by the rabbit-as-ball bouncing through the woods. It seems that the ball as a manifestation of soul has a life or will of its own, an animal life.

> The game now transforms into a mystery of challenges and tricks. The lords challenge the boys to jump over a fire pit. The twins, knowing they are meant to die, sacrifice themselves by jumping into the pit. Their remains are ground up and disposed in a river. They then reappear, first as catfish, and then as humans in the guise of actors. The lords want to see the tricks of the actors, and Xbalanque sacrifices Hunapuh by severing his head and rolling it out the door, removing his heart, and then bringing him back to life. The lords are excited by this and want to try. One and Seven Death are sacrificed, but not brought back to life. Hunapuh and Xbalanque reveal their true identities as heroes and arise into the heavens as the spheres of sun and moon.[1]

In summary, the myth of the *Popol Vuh* provides the ball game with a foundational image depicting a religious mystery having to do with proximity to the underworld, a heroic encounter of play with the gods, the lords of death, ball as autonomous life or soul, sacrifice of life, death as opposition or final goal, and ultimate regeneration.

The Game

> Man plays only when he is in the full sense of the word a man, and he is only wholly man when he is playing.
> —Friedrich Schiller

Evidence exists that the ball game has been played in Central America at least since 1000 B.C. (Ekholm 1991, 242). The game had both sacred and secular functions. In its secular form it was played for recreation and was associated with gambling for material goods, textiles, territory, and even entire empires. In its sacred aspect, the ball game was played as a ritual on courts in the center of religious ceremonial areas. The courts were shaped as the letter *I*, generally 6–12 meters wide and 25–63 meters long. They were surrounded by walls that sloped into the center. There were markers in the courts themselves, and the walls had rings of stone placed perpendicular to the court about 8 feet above the floor. The ball was made of rubber, generally having the proportions of a basketball, weighing 8 pounds. The players of sacred games could be kings, specially trained professionals, or captives, with various numbers to a side—one, two, three, nine, or eleven. The players were equipped with pads protecting the knees and arms, and most important, with a stone yoke that went about the hips. The ball was struck primarily with the hip and also with the buttocks, elbows, and knees, but not with the hands. From the crouched position of players depicted in Mayan art, it would appear the game was played close to the ground. The scoring system was complicated, but the general idea was to keep the ball from hitting the ground on one's own side and to have the ball touch the opponent's ground or touch a marker or ring. A ball going through a ring meant victory for the scoring side, and often the colorful clothing of the spectators would be given to the one who scored.

Perhaps the most intriguing aspect of the Mayan ball game was the sacrificial ritual that accompanied it. It is speculated that at the end of the game a beheading was performed, probably upon the losers or those who had been held captive (Schele 1986, 243). Images of this sacrifice depict the victim, tied up like a ball, rolling down the stairs of the court to where the beheading takes place. Here the mythical theme of play as play-to-death or play against death is literally reenacted as evidenced by the rack of skulls placed adjacent to the ball court. Snakes or plants emerging from the headless body of the victim are depicted in Mayan wall carvings, implying a sense of regeneration in the sacrifice.

The Mayan ball game can be seen in many different ways, each of which provides an archetypal background for contemporary ball games. It served to bring together different components of a community through an event that was out of the realm of ordinary life and that provided community bonding in a sense which Victor Turner calls "communitas" (1969, 96–97). It was a metaphor for combat or war through which kings either celebrated or actually accomplished the winning of territory for their domain.[2] It was a fertility ritual marking the boundaries of the seasons, thus the ball game itself would move the culture over natural thresholds (Gillespie 1991, 330–32). It was a cosmic event in which the king as god or demi-god sets the heavenly bodies on their course, depicted in the soaring ball as the rising of the sun into the heavens and the falling ball as its subsequent descent into the underworld. In the *Popol Vuh*, the appearance of the head of Hunapuh as the ball corresponds with the appearance of Venus in the west, the direction of death.

Finally, the game can be seen as a mode of *initiation* through the ritual acknowledgment of and relationship to the lords of the underworld. In this sense, the ball game becomes the place where death makes its appearance as the final step in the play of life, and where humans have their "close encounter" with the underworld. When we play ball, we are playing against, not only literal death, but the dark forces in our psyches which we think of as "not me," and which strive to have their place in our lives.

The close connection of the ball game with the underworld is revealed in the placement of the ball game on the road to Xibalba at the Place of the Great Abyss, and in the underworld itself against the lords of death. The ball court becomes the gateway to the underworld with the sloping walls of the courts depicting the "jaws of the earth" (Parsons 1991, 197). In addition, the wearing of a stone yoke around the midriff places the player symbolically half in the middleworld and half in the underworld, again a depiction of playing within the jaws of death.

Paralleling the emphasis on the underworld are the images of descent and fall associated with the ball game. The twins' ball and equipment drop from the rafters, the twins descend into the underworld to play, the sacrificial victims were rolled down the stairs to their death, and some of the games took place at the vernal equinox. Each of these descents can be seen as a reflection of the sun's descent into the underworld.

The Mayans, it seems, emphasized the necessity of loss, sacrifice, and death as manifested in the ball game and its background mythical images as central organizing features of life. In the ball game and its sacrifice of beheading lies the experience of suffering and death that is essential for life of the soul. The Mayans seem to be telling us that when there is the experience of death, soul is set into play.

Play as Religious Event

> Man . . . is made God's plaything and that is the best part of him. All of us, then, men and women alike, must fall in with our role and spend life in making our *play* as perfect as possible. . . . Life must be lived as play, playing certain games, that is, sacrifice, song, and dance.
> —Plato, *Laws,* vii, 803

The word "play" comes from the Anglo-Saxon *plega* or *plegan,* meaning both rapid movement and taking a risk or binding or engaging oneself. Similarly, the ancient Greek sense of play included both *paidia,* of or pertaining to a child (improvisation, freedom), and *agon,* having to do with strife or contests. The common root of several Sanskrit words for play contains the image of rapid movement—the movement of wind or waves, shining, sudden appearance, likeness. Likewise the Latin *ludus* is founded on the element of semblance or deception. Play is fundamentally linked with danger, risk, chance, or a feat to which one is bound as if by destiny, ritual, or ceremony, as well as rapid movement, deception, or flashing appearance. There is something serious about play, as well as out of the ordinary, make-believe.

J. Huizinga states that in play there is something "at play" which transcends the immediate needs of life, the appetitive, the rational, the deterministic, but which also imparts meaning to action. Play is based on a particular imagination of reality as separate from the ordinary world. This world is a borderline realm "between jest and earnest" (Huizinga 1949, 5). It has the quality of freedom, yet it is limited in time and space. In sum,

> we might call it (play) a free activity standing quite consciously outside "ordinary" life as being "not serious," but at the same time absorbing the player intensely and utterly. It is an activity connected with no material interest, and no profit can be gained by it. It proceeds within its own proper boundaries of time and space according to fixed rules and in an orderly manner. It promotes the formation of social groupings which tend to surround themselves with secrecy and to stress their difference from the common world by disguise or other means. (Huizinga 1949, 13)

Play functions both as a contest and as a representation. "In the form and function of play, itself an independent entity which is senseless and irrational, man's consciousness that he is embedded in a sacred order of things finds its first, highest and holiest expression" (Huizinga 1949, 17).

The pattern that is created through play, however, is disjunctive—one side wins, one side loses. Disharmony is created in the universe, a disharmony reflected in the severing of the head from the body in the ancient Mayan ritual. The French anthropologist Claude Levi-Strauss refers to this as the "limp" of games as ritual (Levi-Strauss 1973, 460–62). Susan Gillespie (1991, 332–34) considers the "limp" of games as a reflection in time and space of the periodicity of the seasons, ensuring agricultural fertility. From the psychological perspective, however, we would consider disharmony as an inherent *goal* of the play of the world. We want the cosmic order to be symmetrical and harmonious, but the cosmos wants its order disjointed to ensure the movement of soul.

The sense of play as religious ritual revealing a "higher order" would parallel Victor Turner's sense of *liminality*, the condition of being "in between" ordinary and sacred life (Turner 1969, 93–111). Turner refers to Arnold van Gennep's original concept of the *rite de passage* where there is (1) a separation of the sacred from the secular and of the initiate away from the secular; (2) a transition marked by ambiguity and liminality in which the sacred is experienced by the initiate; and (3) incorporation of the initiate, newly informed by the sacred, back into the secular realm (van Gennep 1960). Play as make-believe in earnest would be part of the ludic character of liminality. In other words, play takes place in a sacred ground or *temenos,* outside ordinary time and space yet maintaining certain factors of the familiar. In play there is "a certain freedom to juggle with the factors of existence" (Turner 1967, 106).

Play as religious experience is perhaps best described by Turner when he envisions a factor of "flow" in the player's immersion in liminoid play (Turner 1983, 160–62; Csikszentmihalyi 1990). "Flow" involves the merging of action and awareness in a state of non-selfconsciousness. In flow, there is a centering of attention and limiting of conscious focus so that only "now" matters. Ego as mediator between self and other disappears. The player finds a relationship among self, action, and environment in a way that would not have seemed possible in ordinary situations. Flow contains coherent, noncontradictory demands for action and provides clear, unambiguous feedback to the player's actions. Ultimately, flow needs no goals outside itself. Immersed in flow, the player exists in space and time outside ordinary reality and in service to a "higher order."

Play as Psychological Event

> CLOV: What is there to keep me here?
> HAMM: The dialogue . . .
> CLOV: (*imploringly*): Let's stop playing!
> HAMM: Never!
> —Samuel Beckett

What is this higher order? Huizinga and Turner leave us with play in the ball court of religious event. From the Mayans, however, we have sensed a different order of play—that of soul set into action. To answer this question, we now leave play as a religious event located in the ball court and move out into the streets where play becomes psychological event occurring every moment. The psychological sense of play was formulated by Friedrich Nietzsche throughout his work in both content and style—from the ecstatic playfulness of Dionysus, through the playful aphorism as carrier of knowledge, to playful transformation as a foundation for the major concepts of the Overman, the will to power, and the eternal return. For Nietzsche, play becomes not only the way of associating with great tasks, but also a metaphor for life itself.

George Gadamer (1982) has explicitly revealed play as a fundamental structure of being (see also D. Miller 1970; Hans 1981). Gadamer tells us that play is only play when one loses oneself or is forgetful of oneself (in a condition like Csikszentmihalyi's flow and Turner's liminality). Following Gadamer, all play is "deep play," that is, the player loses subjectivity and play itself becomes the subject (Geertz 1973). Initiative and will are compromised by the subjectivity of play itself, as if both the ball and the game had a separate will or life of their own. If we think of this configuration in terms of the ball game, then the court might be seen as the "body" of the game and the ball as the "soul" or "head" (Gillespie 1991, 338). Experience takes on a life and will of its own, encompassing or playing the player. We will see in chapter 6, for example, how a relationship itself becomes an encompassing third entity that is playing through the two participants as a higher order.

Depth psychology, as part of the postmodern movement, contributes to the project of desubjectivizing experience by positing an "other" or "unconscious" to which subjective consciousness is related. Jung (1961a, 20) related how, as a boy, he sat on a rock and wondered if he was a boy sitting on a rock or the rock imagining a boy on top of it . Following Jung, we might postulate that we are always in a metaphorical existence, that is, living through the form of a larger "other." This other can be a perspective, an ideal, a frame of mind, or a mood, which can be imagined in the form of a container such as a god or goddess, a place, or a text.[3] There is a constant tension between our will or subjectivity and that which is living itself through us. The movement of consciousness back and forth between these two sources might be imagined as play, the to and fro of the hermeneutical circle of consciousness passing back and forth between our attempts to try to gain control of life through understanding and awareness of a larger, more encompassing agent *through which* we are understanding. In terms of the ball game, we have intentionality or purpose, as if we were kicking, throwing, or hitting the ball, but the ball itself also seems to have a will of its own in the service of the game or play in which we are immersed.

This situation of playing while being played with, through a ball that seems to be an object but at the same time has a will of its own, is depicted in the fairy tale, "The Frog King." In the tale, a beautiful princess has a golden ball as a favorite toy with which she plays whenever she becomes bored. As the story goes,

> Now it so happened that on one occasion the princess' golden ball did not fall into the little hand which she was holding up for it, but onto the ground beyond, and rolled straight into the water. (Campbell 1972, 17)

The princess seems to have control of the ball until one day it demonstrates a will of its own, eluding her hand and going directly to its own goal. The story goes on to relate how, from the water, a foreign element can now enter the princess's dry, perfect life in accordance with a higher order.

Gadamer (1982) tells us that the ultimate goal of play is its own presentation or display; the *mode* of play is its self-presentation. In other words, play, or the autonomous body or life, has an inherent form of its own. The intention of play is in the revealing of this form. In the evolution of the form or the pattern of the game, there is a self-remembering. When we sense the form of the game, we see ourselves not as central, rather as only part of a larger picture, an experience of death to the ego and awakening of soul.

The ball game is a reflection of the movement of soul in conjunction with the other, and it is a reflection of our "as if" existence. There is always something going on that we know about, but also something else that we don't know about that brings us down in a fall. We know we have will, but a consciousness that is "more than" us, *has* us as well. We experience the "other" or "more than" subliminally as a kind of death, but it is also the evolving of our creativity and deepening of our being.

The ball is a manifestation of the soul's orientation, bouncing or soaring like the rubber ball of the Mayans, now toward self, now toward other. We are always in a game, a world of both freedom and order within a larger invisible world that is constantly evolving from this play. We are always in some sense in flow, in the self-forgetful experience of the game, intending in one direction, but being played in another. Beckett's character, Hamm, says,

> Old endgame lost of old, play and lose and have done with losing. . . . since that's the way we're playing it . . . let's play it that way . . . and speak no more about it . . . speak no more. (Beckett 1958, 82–84)

Ball/play is the fanciful spirit of the imaginative mode that soul is always falling into, a "text" that speaks us, an image that envelopes us, an archetype that forms us, or a divinity's domain which we inhabit.

As the ball game is a public ritual celebrating the appearance of death, in the next chapter we see how television-watching as a private ritual is an occasion for the appearance of death as the transcendence of the subjective, rational mind.

Finally, ball/play has its own goal of display, and through recognition of play's form played through us, we re-member ourselves in home-coming.

> Catch only what you've thrown yourself, all is
> mere skill and little gain;
> but when you're suddenly the catcher of a ball
> thrown by an eternal partner
> with accurate and measured swing
> towards you, to your centre, in an arch
> from the great bridgebuilding of God:
> why catching then becomes a power—
> not yours, a world's.
>
> —Rilke

CHAPTER FOUR

Spirit in the Tube

The Life of Television

The Soul of Culture

At the time of the invention of television in the early 1920s, the materialist and positivist values of modernism had achieved their zenith. Subjective consciousness lay within the mind and the outer, observable world presented itself as something inanimate—to be measured, controlled, or consumed. Reality was that which was material, public, external, and objectively measurable. The predominant mode of consciousness was rationalism, and spirit was consigned to esoteric group movements.

This state of collective consciousness led many pioneer thinkers of the time to consider the crisis of modern man as being one of the spirit. Jung (1961a, 325) said that the decisive question for the contemporary individual is whether he or she is related to something infinite. Modern man, in his striving for control and certainty, had forgotten a spiritual aspect of the psyche which Jung located in what he called the unknown, "interior" personality or the "unconscious." Consequently, modern man lived a waking death amid what T. S. Eliot called a "heap of broken images," images that Jung saw in the form of myths and symbols concealed in the "inner life" of dreams and fantasies. These myths and symbols, when revealed through analysis, served to unify conscious with unconscious, matter with spirit, and the visible with the invisible, giving a sense of "wholeness" to experience. In other words, Jung's heroic thrust was to stake out ground for "the reality of the psyche," unifying the psyche's disparate aspects into a totality, by delving with the light of consciousness into the dark, inner world of the unconscious personality.

Jung's vision, while focusing on wholeness, still emanated from the ground of modernism, leaving the world as "outer" and inanimate while emphasizing a concealed interior personality as the dwelling-place for the spirit. This mode of thinking, founded on a dualism that interiorizes inherent life or soul and externalizes the world as culture, technology, and nature, is actually an adaptation to a fractured collective consciousness. Culture is seen as impacting analysis which, in turn, is considered as the true agent of change. Cultural factors are imagined as influences on the "psychological development," "dynamics," and "identity" of the individual as interior being. Psychological life is "within" the individual, with the forces of a dead, material world impinging from "without." Culture and psyche are opposed, and care of the soul, or psychotherapy, is an inner work that affects the outer world.

From a different perspective, Jung considered soul to exist prior to notions of within and without. From this position he declared, "psyche is simply 'world'" (Jung 1940, 173). The ideas that psyche does not recognize the distinctions of "within" and "without" and that the world is alive follow in the tradition of *anima mundi* held by native cultures, ancient Greeks, the alchemists of the Middle Ages, and the Neo-Platonists of the Renaissance. *Anima mundi* or the soul of the world is that life which emanates through all perceptible forms. The natural world and the world of technology, as well as the world of dreams and fantasies, have a life of their own. Things of the world show forth their face in their appearance, and in doing so, reveal their depth. Divinity is at work in the machine as well as the dream.

If we follow the spirit of Jung, which was to see soul at work in the dark places of consciousness, and if we now see that psychology harbors a blind spot in relation to the soul of the world, how could we begin to explore the world as psychic reality? What would a psychology of culture be like?

The word "culture" comes from the Latin *cultura,* referring to tilling the soil and the husbandry of animals. It is also associated with care of monuments and training of the body. Culture refers to worship and the observance of rites. It is related to *cultus*—the act of dwelling, training of a person, personal care and adorning, habit.

Care seems to be an important aspect of culture. Care of animals and tilling of land evoke the alchemical notion of working to help nature and to further natural processes. Care for the life of things of the world is religious. The life of the world speaks through things that need us to listen, things that connect us to our past, and not only things—words and ideas as well.

Culture is the meaning given to experience. In Martin Heidegger's (1971) terminology, culture "sets up," "gathers," or "brings forth" a world. Culture provides a dwelling for the world of experience through "careful consideration" or love of ideas, words, things, and experience. The challenge in developing a caring consciousness regarding technological and cultural life would not be to write poetry as an alternative, but to "dwell poetically," to use Heidegger's phrase, with the things of the world.

Culture has its pathologies as part of its poetry. Cultural symptoms are the world's means of calling attention to its needs. One way of imagining the various forms of addiction in contemporary culture would be to consider addiction as a way for subjective consciousness to transcend itself. Dependency on alcohol, drugs, gambling, sex, work, play, and so on, bespeaks the burden of "I-ness" become too great and the need for transcendence of subjectivity. Sleep has traditionally been considered both a metaphor for disenspirited life and a spiritual condition, a place outside "I." The disease of addiction in modern life would then be diagnosed as a "sleep disorder," a yearning for spirit gone wrong, with background images of Dante's and Eliot's crowds of souls living a somnambulate half-life in limbo. We don't know how to meditate, to leave our "selves," to sleep, and so sleep takes us over.

Television as a technological staple of contemporary culture presents itself in just such an ambivalent manner—both as a means for relaxation (transcendence) and as a source of addiction (dysfunction). On one hand, we consider it an essential part of our lives, right up on the needs hierarchy with food, shelter, and the automobile. On the other hand, since its introduction as a popular medium in the late 1940s, it has been regarded with suspicion, often in terms of pathology and addiction. The intent of this chapter is to contribute to a psychology of culture by developing an imagination of television that reveals its concealed life (phenomenology), its myth (Jung), or its "ready-to-hand" essence (Heidegger) as an attempt to transcend subjectivity.

Fallen World

Our relationship to television is marked by a wary attitude regarding its power to influence us. Marshall McLuhan wrote, "It is (the) continuous embrace of our own technology in daily use that puts us in . . . subliminal awareness in relation to these images. . . . [T]hat is why we must . . . serve these objects as gods" (McLuhan 1964, 55). This statement reflects a popular concern for the way television molds our consciousness—our way of thinking, acting, and forming attitudes—as if it were a god (Minnow 1962; Winn 1977; Mander 1978; McCarthy 1990; Tichi 1991; Lazar 1994). The sense of television as a religious power that controls our lives is revealed in the way we relate to it. We pay money for cable television as if in offering, consume products while watching television as if in communion, schedule our day's events around television programming as if in ritual,[1] and become tied to the set when it dramatizes world events as if bending the knee before the altar.

The fear that television controls us is reflected in twentieth-century psychopathology. In 1919, four years before the invention of television, Victor Tausk, a colleague of Freud, wrote an article describing a psychiatric syndrome, a form of delusion, in which patients would characterize themselves as being under the power of an "influencing machine." One of the effects of the machine was seeing pictures on walls, which produced and "drained off" thoughts and feelings by means of waves, rays, or mysterious forces, and "weakened" the patient (Tausk 1967).

In 1959 Dr. Joseph Cowen offered the following description of a woman diagnosed as paranoid schizophrenic:

> For many months during the course of her hospitalization she made frequent reference to television. When she referred to television, she would develop a look of ecstatic terror on her face. In various ways she described how she was being controlled, persecuted and tormented by television. She had clairvoyant experiences with other patients mediated by television. She variously described herself as being "hooked" or "taped" into television. Periodically she would tell me, "Everything would be all right if they just wouldn't turn on the television set." (Cowen 1959, 202–3)

In 1973, a young man walked into the lobby of a San Francisco television station and started shooting a gun in an attempt to shut down the broadcasts. The man thought that a receiver for the waves transmitted by the station had been secretly planted in his body so that it broadcast incessantly to his mind.

The symptomatology of these modern psychiatric patients can be seen as a reflection of the "dis-ease" of our culture. Their symptoms might be seen as the condition of a culture unduly "under the influence" of an objectivizing, analytic, "far-seeing" (tele-vision) eye that has come to take on a persecutory character.

Our ambivalence toward television-watching stems, in part, from the dark connotation it carries through its association with addiction. Marie Winn called television "the plug-in drug." Jack Gould, the first television critic of the *New York Times*, in 1948 referred to television as an "insidious narcotic" (Winn 1977, 11). Robert D. McIlwraith of the University of Manitoba states that the main attraction of television-watching is not the content of programming, but a dependency on the medium itself. Robert Kubey of Rutgers University found through his research that (1) television-watching alters mood states; (2) television-watching can be compared to substance addiction in that it is used more than intended; (3) people recognize that their use of television is often excessive but are unable to control it; (4) important social activities are given up or reduced in favor of television-watching; and (5) withdrawal symptoms develop when an individual stops or reduces viewing (McCarthy 1990, 42).

The volume of television-watching in the United States might be seen as indicative of an addiction. It is estimated by the Smithsonian Institute that in the average American household a television set is on 7.5 hours per day. The average American spends 4.4 hours per day watching television (Edwards 1997). The average preschool child watches television about 28 hours per week, and the average elementary school age child watches 24 hours per week (Lazar 1994, 67). By the completion of high school, a child can be expected to have watched 15,000 hours of television—far more than the child's accumulated hours of classroom time and more than any other activity except sleep (*Esquire,* 122).

From its inception, television has been presented not only as a medium of entertainment, but also as a medium of education wherein the world is brought into the living room. However, little factual information is actually remembered from television-watching. Instead, television images tend to pour through consciousness, bypassing the cognitive faculties. One woman who, at 20, estimated that she had watched twenty thousand hours of television, confided, "it all just washed over me" (Winn 1977, 10). Even so-called educational programs do not enhance learning in children unless they are accompanied by adult intervention (Winn 1977, 34). Research from Australia indicates that television destroys the capacity of the viewer to attend (Mander 1978, 14). While the medical world has created a psychiatric diagnostic category of attention deficit disorder in children and adults, Winn suggests that it is television-watching that inhibits left-brain development and the ability to concentrate necessary for achievement in literary education and cognitive development (Winn 1977, 43–44). Bonnie Lazar cites evidence that heavy television watching can cause increased restlessness as well as aggression in children and that viewing television consistently can cause a replacement of imaginative play with imitative play (Lazar 1994, 68).

Disillusionment regarding television extends to its sociological as well as its psychological effects. While television-watching was originally imagined as a family and community event, gathering the group around the hearth (Tichi 1991), in fact it has replaced rituals of family and community life such as the evening dinner and neighborly chats. Each individual family member now is more likely to commune with a private television set in his or her room (or, as in Japan, each individual in a room with his or her individualized television set and a pair of earphones). Even the ritual of viewing of the dead is now accomplished in distanced solitude by means of drive-in television at mortuaries. From this perspective, television-watching can be seen as a symptom of our time, rendering the individual confined to isolated existence, poorly equipped to initiate connection and interact with the world.

The moralistic flavor of dialogue regarding television reflects not only our ambivalence, but a spiritual conflict of good versus evil (Minnow 1962). Television is often described as if it were something sinister, a technological Cyclops consuming our minds, a tool in the hands of group-think engineers who market the raw material of culture—things, ideas, words, and experience—as commodities to be bought and sold. Television would be viewed as having replaced the world, becoming a world in itself, a world without substance, a world of glowing, fuzzy, phosphorescent, electric dots. From this perspective, television would be seen as tricking us into thinking that it "brings the busy world before us," or "mirrors the sights of life," as it was originally advertised to do. Television would seem to have taken over imagination and become, for the modern individual, a mass anesthetic, a universal medicine show, a global baby-sitter. Mass television-watching would be seen as Huxley's "brave new world" where people love servitude to invisible authority through greatly improved techniques of suggestion. Television would seem to have taken us into Orwell's "1984," where a television screen in every room exists in perpetual vigilance of the individual, where human consciousness is engineered by technicians of "goodthink," and where the worst horror is that no one realizes their condition of servitude because the oppressors remain invisible. In sum, television would be the shadow of Yeats' prophecy that the visible world is no longer a reality and the unseen world is no longer a dream.

As the weight of the moral attitude regarding television becomes overbearing, the question turns back on itself. Might not the very morality of our discussion regarding television reflect something of its essence? Would not this moral stance indicate a hidden inherent spiritual dimension to television? In that case, television could be imagined as a god, not because of our unconsciousness, but its own self-presentation. Television would be seen as having a spiritual life of its own.

If this is the case, then we might ask: What would be its hidden intention and how have we failed to respond adequately to the calling within television's presence?

Television as Aphrodite

To be sure, television does exercise a form of subliminal control, an influence that might also be described as hypnotic. The actual experience of watching television can be likened to that of a trance state. Consciousness becomes desensitized to emotions and the perception of things and sounds. The eyes become still and the body quiets to the flickering light. People describe themselves as being "hooked," "doped," "sucked in," "fixated," "zombie-like," "dependent," and "suggestible." The sense of time becomes distorted, experience in the world seems unreal, and there is an inability to discriminate. This hypnotic effect of the television image is inherent in the physiology of television-watching.

Scientists interested in brain waves characterize television-watching as an activity with a high percentage of alpha-wave activity, which is associated with the relaxed, unfocused, inner-directedness of consciousness. (Beta-wave activity is characteristic of an outer focus.) In addition, perception is normally characterized by a small percentage of activity in the fovea, the sharp-focusing part of the eye. We take in the greater part of the world through peripheral vision. In watching television, by contrast, the eye tends to focus exclusively on the screen, taking in the entire image through the fovea, leaving the peripheral world blotted out. This is because the televised image produces contours that are always moving, and the eye is drawn to fixate on these moving contour lines. The contours of objects in the world are then perceived as stationary. When the eye attempts to adjust to the constantly changing image of television, the result is a defocusing of the visualizing system. The constantly changing contour of the televised image stimulates a mechanism of adjustment wherein the eye defocuses in an attempt to fixate properly. The defocusing of the eye, in effect, tunes out the world and brings about an hypnotic state of consciousness.

As McLuhan has pointed out, television as a medium attracts consciousness into the screen itself. "It is the total involvement in all-inclusive *nowness* that occurs in young lives via TV's mosaic image" (McLuhan 1964, 292). When we are watching television, we are not seeing the natural world as we are led to believe, or even a projected image as in film, but a mosaic of patterns formed by 300,000 phosphorescent dots flickering every second. This mosaic requires an unconscious "creation," an interpretation or selection process on the part of the viewer. The creation of image is really not that, however, since the image is already formed for us. Rather it is a kind of subliminal "painting by the numbers" or "connecting the dots" which actually deprives us of imagination. Nevertheless, it is an action that unconsciously draws us into the television screen, impelling us to be "with it." (In addition, technical effects such as the quick cuts in advertisements have a special attraction for the observing eye.)

The hypnotic attraction of the televised image is a sensuous attraction, affecting our tactile perception and extending our sense of touch. McLuhan suggests that because the television image is the result of light shining through, not on, a screen, it has the experiential quality of sculpture. We can also see that the televised image lies in the tradition of impressionistic painting which immediately preceded its invention. The impressionists remind us of the bodily existence of the world by bringing us into a tactile relationship with the painted image. Cezanne said that we should paint as if we held things in our hands, not as if we were observing them. He abandoned linear perspective in favor of structure created with small strokes of the brush. Seurat achieved a similar effect with dots on the canvas. Seeing mythologically, we might view this sensuous attraction of the television screen as Aphrodite asking for bodily interaction.

In attempting to understand the psychological intention of television removing us from the control of our reasoning mind, we have characterized television as a medium of the senses. As a technology of the sensuous, television draws us out of our subjective mind. Subjectivism is an attitude which says the *source* of consciousness is within the individual human mind, and consciousness is separate from the surrounding world. To understand further the psychological necessity of "losing our minds" and the inherent connection between television and subjectivism, we now need to look historically at the background of subjectivism and imagine its connection to television. In the next section, I attempt to show how television evolves out of the subjectivist mind, starting with a brief review of the evolution of subjectivism from the invention of linear perspective during the Renaissance (Edgerton 1976; Romanyshyn 1989).

Tele-vision as Subjectivist Mind

At the root of subjectivism are two ideas that came together and became predominant during the Renaissance: (1) the universe is ordered according to laws of harmony or proportion, and (2) earthly order reflects heavenly order. The fundamental principle of the first idea, proportion, is that the concrete, particular fragment can be understood in terms of an encompassing unity through a mathematically predictable order in the relationship of its parts. In other words, each entity relates to a greater whole through a numerical order. Proportion, based as it is on numbers, is concerned with quantity, as opposed to quality, and concepts, as opposed to images. The spiritual basis of proportion can be seen in the thought of one of its founders, the Greek theologian and mathematician Pythagoras. Pythagoras believed that a purely spiritual existence could be achieved through the progression of the soul through the inherent levels of order in the universe from matter to spirit, each based on number. He held that all things of the universe, such as the notes on a musical scale, are ordered through the numerical distribution of their elements. For Pythagoras, things were not substantial in themselves, but were essentially numbers!

A second classical idea that found a receptive place in the Renaissance mind was that order on earth reflects heavenly order: "as above, so below." If heavenly order is proportionate, then earthly order must be proportionate as well. During the Renaissance, proportion as metaphysical system became transformed into linear perspective as methodology. The "ground" of earthly reality came to be not something that was unknowable because it rested in the mind of God. Rather, earthly reality became that which could be observed from a fixed point through the application of linear perspective, and mathematics was its ground.

Linear perspective was invented by Filippo Brunelleschi (1374–1446), a Florentine painter and designer, when he painted the exact likeness of the doorway to the baptistery in Florence from its image in a mirror. *Perspectiva* is a Latin word that means "a view through something." With linear perspective, that "something" is a *transparent window* through which we look out onto a section of the visible world," as expressed by the Renaissance theoretician of art and architecture, Leon Battista Alberti (Panofsky 1955, 247, italics mine).

Brunelleschi invented perspective by connecting two premises. The first is that the visual image is produced by straight lines that connect the eye with objects so that the resulting configuration becomes a pyramid, with the eye forming the apex and the horizon forming the base (fig. 1). The second is that the size and shape of the objects in the image are determined by the relative position of the rays that make them visible (fig. 2). The closer an object to the eye, the larger it will be. Brunelleschi's revolutionary idea

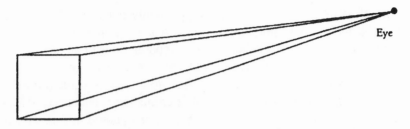

Figure 1. The Visual Pyramid.

Figure 2. Vision and Proportion.

was to conceive of a plane being interjected between the eye and the horizon, allowing for the projection of the visual image onto this surface by calculating numerically where the rays will intersect the plane (fig. 3). The effect was that "you thought you saw the proper truth and not an image" (de Santillana 1969, 64).

The theory of linear perspective is based upon the assumption by the viewer that through proportion, large things can be represented as smaller. The truth of an object becomes, not the quality of its form, but its *measure* both in size and in distance from the viewer. Objects diminish in size as their distance from the beholder increases. The laws of proportion allowed for the possibility of linear perspective, in that, with proportion, what appeared small signified distance and what appeared large signified close proximity. With perspective, "reality" was no longer the ideal image in the soul, but that which was literal, known through sensory perception, and objectively measurable. Reality became a three-dimensional space, composed of objects and interstices that seemed to extend indefinitely behind the proscenium "frame" of the visual image. Again, I would suggest that the proscenium frame of linear perspective, which started out on the Renaissance painter's

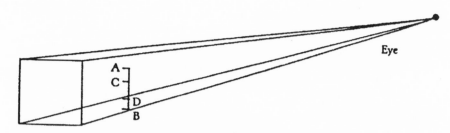

Figure 3. The Visual Plane of Linear Perspective.

canvas as "window to the world," can be imagined as a forerunner of the television screen, once advertised as "the biggest window in the world."

The achievement of linear perspective, as the metaphysics of proportion literalized, had several important psychological implications (Romanyshyn 1989). Consciousness became distanced from the world, fixed, flattened, and singular. The further the observer was detached from the world, the greater the sense of proportion and the more vision became "truth" as mathematical order, the more individual consciousness became the seat of judgment. The vanishing point in linear perspective, that is, the center of the image that draws focus to itself, might be imagined as reflecting the "divine eye" of God. This eye was now replaced by the observing eye of the individual (figs. 4 and 5). It was a short jump to the advent of subjectivism through Descartes' relocating the seat of all consciousness in the mind of humans—"I think, therefore I am." The world became dis-ensouled, something inorganic that was perceived most accurately, not through actual experience, but as if through a window. In the Renaissance, life became, as with television today, a form of peep show seen through a magic window (fig. 6).

When soul, the classical union of spirit and matter, is withdrawn from the world into the mind, spirit and matter become split from each other. Spirit becomes linked to faith in an unseen realm, matter becomes inorganic, and the world becomes dead. There is set up in the soul a yearning for spirit and body unified, a desire for an ensouled "world" with its own life.

Today the subjectivist mind continues to keep matter and spirit separate. We think that television brings the world as literal reality into our homes, just as Renaissance man thought of reality as revealed through the boxed-in window of linear perspective. Detached from the world, we use television to bring us the world, but what we actually witness are preformed matrixes of artificial light brought to us from a singular perspective.

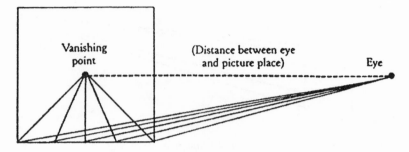

Figure 4. The Vanishing Point of Linear Perspective.

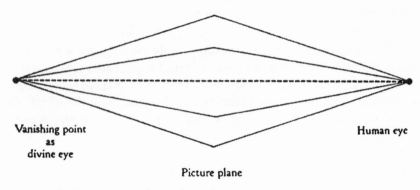

Figure 5. The Detached Eye and the Divine Eye.

In providing an alternative understanding of television, I would suggest that television, when seen as an entity with a life or essence that has an intention of its own, is a response to the soul's need to transcend subjectivity and unify the material "reality" of the modern world with spirit.

Spirit in the Tube

Walter Ong has specified three different technological stages in the evolution of communication: the oral tradition, the written tradition of script and print, and the electronic tradition of television and computers (Ong 1967, 1982). Each change in stage has brought with it a crisis, the older paradigm being highly suspect of the newer. For instance, through the voice of Socrates (*Phaedrus* 275–76), Plato voiced objections to writing that are similar to contemporary objections to television. He asserted that writing was an inhuman form of interaction, attempting to establish outside the

Figure 6. Renaissance Observers. From The Medium Is the Massage, *by Marshall McLuhan and Quentin Fiore (New York: Bantam Books, 1967).*

mind what in reality can only be in the mind, that writing destroys memory, and that writing is passive and unresponsive.

What seems to be required during each crisis is a dramatic leap in imagination. I have proposed that the television-watching eye is an analogue to the subjective eye of modernity, which itself is an analogue to the divine eye of the Middle Ages. I have also stated that the subjectivist mind, as an analogue to the mind of God, is blind to autonomous life outside itself, leaving it perpetually in search of soul through spiritual awakening. I now suggest that television, as a product of the subjectivist eye that came about in time of spiritual crisis, has an inherent life within it that would transcend subjectivism through spiritual connection. In other words, television-watching has an underlying intention toward religious experience.

From the derivation of the word, "tele-vision" bespeaks Apollo, the far-shooting god of light. *Tele* in Greek means "at a distance" or "far off." "Vision" comes from the Latin word for the act of seeing, which in turn, comes from the Greek *eidos,* referring to that which is seen or known. For the Greeks, direct perception of appearance was knowing. Television is "seeing or knowing at a distance."

The light of television is not the clear, bright sunlight of Apollo, however. It takes on more of the quality of the glow of his equally far-shooting sister, the moon goddess, Artemis. We might say that the soft light of television is a form of "moonshine," with television-watching taking on the aspect of moon-gazing, peering into a mist, or being drawn toward the feminine mysteries.

The light of television can be considered as a form of "divine light" when we look at how it evolved and how it works. In 1884, Paul Nipkow, a German scientist, invented a small disc with holes, which, when rotated, broke up the image of an object into light waves. He then converted the different strengths of light waves from the object into electrical impulses of corresponding strengths through photosensitive selenium cells (discovered in 1873). Nipkow theorized that by using another scanning device, these impulses could be converted back into an image of the original object. This step in the evolution of television was accomplished with the invention of the electric cathode ray tube by William Crookes in 1897.

The motivation behind Crookes's discovery reveals the spiritual element in television. Crookes had been interested in bridging the gap between the physical and spiritual worlds all his life. He claimed at one point to have photographed the manifestation of a spirit conjured by a medium in his laboratory. In particular, he longed to communicate with his dead brother and was quite attracted to the notion that electricity, when passed through rarefied gases, could create mediumistic effects. (We see this dramatized in old Frankenstein movies in the secret laboratory where electrical charges, passing through gases creating spectacular effects, evoke life in the corpse on the table.) Instead, Crookes discovered a "borderland where Matter and Force seem to merge into one another" (Lehrs 1985, 58). The eventual result was the invention of the cathode ray tube, where an image was produced by electrons when electricity passed through a pressurized container of gases.

In the early 1920s, John Logie Baird, a British inventor, produced the first telecasts using a mechanical device similar to that developed by Nipkow.

Campbell Swinton, a British scientist, and Boris Rosing, a Russian, each replaced the mechanical scanning device with the electric cathode ray tube. With the cathode ray tube, an image could be picked up on a thin plate coated with a photosensitive substance. This plate was bombarded with electrons "shot" from a "gun" at the other end of the tube. The fusillade, sweeping up and down and from side to side, provided electrical impulses matching the image being received on the plate. These impulses were, in turn, transmitted to a receiver that converted them back into light rays which were projected, this time onto a fluorescent screen.

Television is produced when light from objects is broken up, converted into electrical impulses, transmitted to a distant receiver, reconverted to light rays, and finally projected onto a screen made up of thousands of phosphorescent nodules that glow when stimulated. When we watch television, we are watching what happens when a 25,000 volt cathode ray gun, going off at the rate of 30 times per second, shoots impulses onto a screen made up of 300,000 dots packed into 500 lines. Keeping in mind the intention behind Crookes's discovery, it is as if, through television-watching, we are affected by a tremendous act of penetration from "without" or from an unseen realm.

In approaching television imaginatively as an attempt at connection with a spiritual world, a scene from Dante's *Paradiso* provides a sense of the divine world making itself manifest to the human eye through a matrix of lights. In the Eighteenth Canto, Dante is following his guide, Beatrice, through the heavenly realm of Justice illuminated by the star of Jupiter. Here he sees two images formed by configurations of the glowing lights of angelic souls. Dante tells us, "within the lights, holy creatures were singing as they flew and made themselves, in the figures they formed." The angels first formed themselves into letters that spelled the Latin words for "Love Justice, ye that love the earth." Then Dante declares that he saw the head and neck of an eagle, the bird of justice, represented in the "pricked-out fire." Dante's vision of the "pricked-out fire" could be imagined as the first televised image. In the early Renaissance, Dante saw figures formed by glowing angels; today, we might imagine our angels as electrically activated, glowing, phosphorescent dots making up the figures in the televised image.

To further help make the imaginal leap connecting television and spirit, the history of interrelationship between spirit and electricity presents itself. Electricity has been associated with spirit from the beginning of recorded time. Zeus was thought to cast his thunderbolts as a form of divine judgment. It is possible that ancient Mediterranean peoples used pools of electric fish as a form of electroshock therapy (Benz 1989, ix).

By the eighteenth century, electricity was considered by many physicians as intrinsic to the life processes of both animals and humans.

In the alchemy of the late Renaissance, electricity was considered the "ethereal fire" or the "quintessential fire" (Benz 1989, x), and it became the primary image for the presence of divine power in the world. Anton von Balthasar wrote in 1745 of the Pentecost as "spiritual electrisation" and interpreted the Holy Ghost's Pentecostal tongues of fire as electricity (Benz 1989, 40). Prokop Divisch (1696–1765), who wrote the first document in German scientific literature on electricity, and Gottlieb Rosler (1740–90), his interpreter, were both scholars of religion and science who held that the light of the first day of creation described in Genesis 1:3 was the "electrical fire" added to matter. Friedrich Oetinger, a contemporary of Divisch and the founder of the theosophical movement, expanded this notion into a complete electrical theology. In this theology, which combined biblical revelation and the natural sciences, the electrical fire, as life spirit, spread out over chaos as matter, stimulating, warming, and finally fusing with it. The "electrical fire concealed in all things" is the life principle that again and again manifests itself by penetrating new forms. Ever since the Creation, life has been bestowed upon matter in a secret concealed impulse. Oetinger and Divisch considered this life source the soul, the nature of which was "analogous to electrical phenomena." This soul was termed the "animal soul" as distinct from the more overt "rational soul" of the mind. It is through the animal soul that spirit and matter come together, that body and psychic functions cohere. From the standpoint of alchemy, it is in the electrical fire of the animal soul wherein dwells the a priori unity of spirit and matter, today manifested in the televised image.

If electricity can be imagined as a modern form of divine fire, stolen from the heavens by Benjamin Franklin (Bennet 1985), and the television image as its concrete manifestation, might not the television set be the contemporary hearth—television as Hestia (Tichi 1991)? The hearth evokes the age-old tradition of storytelling which takes us back to our origins. The image of the hearth emerges in the early fantasies of the purveyors of television, who imagined the whole family gathered about the television set in the evening much as it might gather around the stove or the fireplace. The matrix of glowing nodules of the televised image draws consciousness into it, reminiscent of the attraction of the embers of a fire. The act of gazing into a matrix of glowing luminaries can be imagined as a form of the ancient art of contemplation, the careful consideration of that which is eternal or beyond the grasp of man, that is, the "divine light." Gaston Bachelard describes fire-gazing as a meditative phenomenon or reverie that allows "the grieving soul to give voice to its memories and sorrows" (Bachelard 1964, 3). Fire-gazing is a common form of divination in native cultures. In the Navajo culture, medical diagnoses are made by gazing into the coals of the fire. So when we are watching television, we are enacting a tradition of imagining, storytelling, and remembering and we are repeating a meditative, contemplative ritual of connection with what is beyond mortal comprehension.

Television-watching as engagement of the unconscious through hypnotic means gives evidence to the soul's yearning for sleep (Hypnos). "Sleep," here, can be imagined as the "ego-lessened" state wherein subjective consciousness loses its grip on the psyche. In the Buddhist mind, sleep is simply the state when heaviness and stability are increased. It is a time of stopping, when there is no desire. Chuang Tzu taught that everything is one in sleep, and the legendary Hindu hero/king, Mucukunda, chose a life of perpetual sleep after his exploits were finished. For the ancient Greeks, sleeping was the time when healing would occur through contact with a divinity in dreams. When Western mythical heroes from Gilgamesh to Ulysses to Samson to Jesus fall asleep, something psychologically important happens.

Mythically, sleep and death are connected, Hypnos and Thanatos as brothers. Friedrich Nietzsche said that all that is right seeks death, Freud considered the desire for death to be an instinct, and Jung saw death as life's goal. The soul yearns for death, and Bachelard connects fire-gazing with this desire. He writes:

> [F]ire suggests the desire to change, to speed up the passage of time, to bring all life to its conclusion, to its here-after. In these circumstances the reverie becomes truly fascinating and dramatic; it magnifies human destiny; it links the small to the great, the hearth to the volcano, the life of a log to the life of a world. The fascinated individual hears the call of the funeral pyre. For him destruction is more than a change, it is a renewal.
>
> This very special and yet very general kind of reverie leads to a true complex in which are united the love and the respect for fire, the instinct for living and the instinct for dying. (Bachelard 1964, 16)

Bachelard names this complex the "Empedocles complex" after the Greek philosopher who chose a death through fire, the element he thought of as fundamental, by hurling himself into a volcano. For Bachelard, the soul yearning for death through reverie is drawn by the fire to be swallowed up and to disappear into a condition in which "the universe is reduced to nothingness" (Bachelard 1964, 13). In this sense, contemporary television-watching would be a response to the soul's yearning for death, the yearning for unity with infinity through the fascinated gaze into, and ultimate engulfment by, the fire glowing in the screen.

We watch television; television watches us. McLuhan says, "TV is environmental and imperceptible, like all environments" (McLuhan 1964, ix). We have found that, seen through psychological vision, television is a world encompassing us with a life of its own. Following alchemy and Jung, I am suggesting that the intention of this life is to unite spirit or invisible life with material or visible life to make psychological "image." The act of television-watching then becomes an attempt to transcend the tyranny of subjective "I-ness" through contemplation, sleep, and death. This attempt has been aborted by a collective consciousness that has maintained a subjective attitude and literal imagination regarding television, using it as an agent of its own purposes, rather than recognizing the god in technology, the spirit in the tube.

We have seen that ball play and television-watching are subliminal rituals of encounter with death. The next two chapters on fathers and sons and relationship deal with the conscious experience of death in our everyday lives.

PART THREE

Death as Experience

CHAPTER FIVE

Fathers and Sons

The Perpetual Circling Storm

> Fatherhood, in the sense of conscious begetting, is
> unknown to man. It is a mystical estate, an apostolic
> succession, from only begetter to only begotten. On that
> mystery . . . the church is founded . . . like the world,
> macro- and microcosm, upon the void.
>
> —Joyce, *Ulysses*

The Oedipal and the Absent Father

The view of fathers and sons as being inherently in conflict has come to
be one of the pillars of contemporary psychology. It is aptly expressed by
anthropologist Weston Labarre:

> The relation of fathers and sons is mysterious and terrifying. It
> has never been rational, nor will it ever be. . . . Father and son
> form the most critical and dangerous animal relationship on earth,
> and to suppose otherwise is to invite catastrophe. For it is by no
> means delivered to us that this species-paradigm will survive
> annihilation in blind self-slaughter through some displaced path-
> ology of this relationship. No man ever grows beyond the reach
> of its influence. (Esman 1981, 265)

LaBarre is expressing a view that is derived from the work of one of the
fathers of our time, Sigmund Freud. Freud delineated an orientation toward
fathers and sons that gave dramatic expression to insights derived from his
self-analysis after the death of his own father. It is an ambivalent model,
including both love and hostility. The emphasis on hostility comes from the
idea, based on the myth of Oedipus, that the son experiences the father as a
rival for possession of the mother, has impulses to get rid of the father, is
fearful of castration by the father and gives up his wishes, and eventually

identifies with the father as a form of surrender. Here, the only channels available for intimacy between fathers and sons are through competition and punishment. Fathers present themselves as competitors and authorities to be overcome, the father/son relationship becomes a struggle for power, and sons survive only through a compromise formation—"I can't overcome Dad, but at least I can be like him."

Fathers have not had it very good with sons for other reasons. Whereas fathers have been resented for their control, rigidity, or cruel punishment, they have also been grieved over for their absence, distance, or coldness. Fathers' absence—absent-mindedness, behind the newspaper or in front of the television, off at work or to the committee meeting, "under the influence"—breeds sadness in sons. Fathers are laughed at for their foolishness or held in contempt for their betrayal. A passage from a talk by the poet, Robert Bly, describes the condition of the contemporary father.

> I meet young fathers who do not know what male values they should attempt to teach their sons. These men, often separated from their own remote fathers, and out of touch with their grandfathers, do not feel they belong to a community of men. When they reach out toward truly masculine values, they find nothing in their hand when it closes.
>
> The old anger against the father . . . has been replaced in many men by a kind of passivity and remoteness, which springs from a feeling that the father has abandoned or rejected them. . . . One feels in these men a longing for male values mingled with a kind of helpless bitterness. (Bly 1987, 189–90)

Likewise, the priest, Henri Nouwen, spells out the problem of the loss of authority which the father has traditionally provided.

> The last one to be listened to is father. We are facing a generation which has parents but no fathers, a generation in which everyone who claims authority—because he is older, more mature, more intelligent or more powerful—is suspect from the very beginning. (Nouwen 1972, 30)

Alexander Mitschedlich (1973) has written on American society without father, pointing out that America was born out of rebellion against the father as unjust monarch. Politically, the making of America demanded that the father be rejected and modified as a source of authority. In addition, the technical developments brought about by the Industrial Age eliminated the opportunity for the workplace to be a venue for father to pass his craft on to his son. A son could no longer watch father while working with him, see the way he handled things, and observe the degree of knowledge and skill the father had attained. The depersonalization of work made father's livelihood invisible to the son and left the father with no tangible creation to bring home. Father's authority through work became eroded, resulting in the diminution of his place in the family. As work became more abstract, father could no longer teach the ability to concentrate, the pleasure of contact with physical things, the satisfaction of putting one's individual stamp on a product, and such creative qualities as decisiveness, a sense of craft and work values, and discriminatory judgment.

Conflict and absence, however, are not just modern manifestations of the father/son configuration. On the one hand, fathers have always been rough and rigid. Rumi wrote in Persia in the fifteenth century,

> Your old grandmother says,
> "Maybe you shouldn't go to school.
> You look a little pale."
> Run when you hear that.
> A father's stern slaps are better.
> Your bodily soul wants comforting.
> The severe father wants spiritual clarity.
> He scolds, but eventually
> leads you into the open.
> (Bly, Hillman, and Meade 1992, 136)

On the other hand, fathers have always been called away by the spirit of work or war. Rilke wrote,

> Sometimes a man stands up during supper
> and walks outdoors, and keeps on walking,
> because of a church that stands somewhere in the East.
> And his children say blessings on him as if he were dead.
> And another man, who remains inside his own house,
> dies there, inside the dishes and in the glasses,
> so that his children have to go far out into the world
> toward the same church, which he forgot.
> (Bly, Hillman, and Meade 1992, 60)

If we look at images in our Western mythical, religious, and literary tradition of fathers and sons, images that form the foundation for our experience of this relationship, we find that conflict and absence are the very qualities which dominate the archetypal landscape. In other words, there seems to be something enduring, something of intention or necessity in the hostility and distance between father and son.

In the *Theogony,* Hesiod (800–700 B.C.) tells how the sky god, Ouranos, imprisons his children in the womb of their mother, Gaia, the earth. The youngest of these is "devious-devising Kronos," who hates his strong father. In collusion with his mother, Kronos castrates Ouranos. Kronos, in turn, becomes as tyrannical as his father. Hearing that it has been ordained for him to be overthrown by his own son, Kronos swallows all of his children. However, Rheia, his sister and consort, hides Zeus, the youngest child, and replaces him with a stone which Kronos swallows. Zeus grows up to his full capabilities in secret, eventually overthrowing his father with the help of his freed siblings and the Titans, casting Kronos into the depths. Zeus, in turn, is warned that he will be overthrown by his son, and swallows his pregnant wife Metis.

These stories present an image of stifling and devouring fathers frightened by the possibilities of sons, and rebellious sons colluding with mothers against fathers, resulting in castration, depotentiation, banishment, or distancing of fathers. Age stands in opposition to youth, depression to joy, form to freedom, law to imagination, and experience to innocence. The quality of relationship is one of competition, conflict, challenge, deceit, and violence. At the same time, it is as if these are the conditions required for the emergence of the individuality in each new generation to take place. James Hillman, the contemporary depth psychologist, has written most profoundly on the subject (1970, 1975a, b, 1979 a, b, 1987a, 1997b), saying that whatever lies in the path of any son, whether Oedipus or Siegfried, *fathers* the son. "Father too is impelled by archetypal necessity to isolate, ignore, neglect, abandon, expose, disavow, devour, enslave, sell, maim, betray the son" (Hillman 1987a, 278).

The Judeo-Christian tradition offers a variation on the theme of conflict and distance between father and son. After his father dies Abraham is told by his spiritual father, Yahweh, that he will be blessed if he leaves the home of his father, and Abraham obeys. He moves from the domain of the literal father to join in relationship with the spirit father who has greater value. Distance is necessary for allegiance to a more encompassing level of authority. This father is unseen and distant, but the relationship is one of care and blessing on the part of father and obedience and readiness to do father's will on the part of the son.

Abraham questions Yahweh and bargains with him regarding the destruction of Sodom and Gomorrah. In doing so he brings dialogue to the father/son image. The word "dialogue" means "for logos" and *logos* means "causes to come into being." Existence unfolds through a pattern of speaking back and forth between father and son.

Abraham's first son, Ishmael, born to his wife's serving lady, Hagar, is banished along with his mother—a distancing from father—but Ishmael eventually returns to help bury his father. When Abraham's second son, Isaac, is a boy, Yahweh calls Abraham and Abraham responds, "Here I am." He is present to Yahweh and ready to do his will. Yahweh instructs Abraham to take his beloved son and offer him as a sacrifice. The father's killing of the son is presented as a religious event, a sacrifice, the giving up of the most prized possession for a higher order. When Isaac calls his father, Abraham again says, "Here I am," his ready presence a conduit to both father and son. Isaac queries his father, "Where is the lamb?" There is always a sacrifice; the question is, Who is to be the victim? Abraham's response is that God will provide the sacrificial lamb. Sacrifice is part of God's will, and father and son go together to do His bidding. Separation and sacrifice are part of father/son togetherness.

Isaac has twin sons, Esau, the red, hairy, hunter and man of the field, Isaac's favorite, and Jacob, the plain man who dwells in tents and is his mother's favorite. Esau returns his father's favoritism with loyalty and consideration, but loses his birthright to Jacob in exchange for sustenance. Jacob, in collusion with his mother, deceives his father, now blind, into giving him his blessing. Again, father needs to be deceived into granting the son his individual existence, and again, mother is involved in the deception. Esau as heir and firstborn son is sacrificed, losing birthright and first blessing.[1]

Frightened by the threat of Esau's revenge, Jacob leaves Isaac to procure a wife. He works for his maternal uncle, Laban, in pursuit of Laban's daughter, Rachel, and is deceived by Laban, just as he deceived his father. His service to Laban stretches into an initiation period of twenty years. Finally Jacob is visited by God in a dream and responds, "Here I am," again, the son in readiness for the spirit father. God tells Jacob to return, and he attempts to leave Laban by sneaking away. Laban catches up and there is negotiation, again dialogue. A settlement is worked out, a covenant is made, and Jacob returns to his homeland. Although there is deception between fathers and sons, the deception is revealed to have necessity about it. A son is sacrificed, a son moves away from the father, son and new father negotiate, and a son comes into his own individuality.

Jacob has twelve sons, the youngest of which is Joseph, the favorite of Jacob, to whom Jacob gave a coat of many colors. Fathers invest sons with the colors of life and with a plurality of values and emotional attitudes that shape an individual's life (Beebe 1986). Joseph's brothers conspire against him, and he is sold into slavery, after which he is accused of taking his master's place in the marital bed, again a form of father/son rivalry. Ultimately, Joseph emerges as a confidant and advisor to the Pharaoh, essentially fathering the father. Joseph becomes ruler, is reunited with his brothers, and asks them to bring his father, Jacob. Jacob blesses Joseph's two sons before he dies.

These Old Testament stories of fathers and sons go on through David and the rebellion of his son Absalom into the New Testament and the mission of Jesus for his Father. Jesus ends his earthly life, confronting his father in agony with the ultimate question of betrayal by the father, "My God, my God, why hast thou forsaken me!"

What do the biblical stories of struggles between fathers and sons tell us? From the standpoint of the son, the primal condition of trust is unity with the father—this is the beginning point (Adam in the Garden) and the goal (the reuniting of God the Father and Jesus the Son). Fathers are unjust, but a betrayal is called for as initiation into an inherently unjust life (Hillman 1975a). The father's curse is also a blessing. Dylan Thomas:

> And you my father, there on the sad height
> Curse, bless me now with your fierce tears I pray.
> (Thomas 1963)

At the same time, sons say to fathers, "Here I am," ready to assume responsibility amid danger in service to the father (Wiesel 1976). The word "patriarch" comes from the Greek *patriarchos,* meaning "father of a race." Our word "rule" comes from the Latin *regulare,* from *regula* which is a straight piece of wood, and our word "pattern" comes from the Latin *patris,* or "father." The father is the straight piece of wood or the established pattern or habit from which the son needs to bend, stretch, or break apart. The Old Testament patriarchs struggled with famine, drought, adverse neighbors, rivalrous kin, temptations, and a demanding God, and through their diplomacy and ultimate survival, founded a nation. They evolved a mode that employed knowledge, cunning, alert awareness, practicality, planning, ingenuity, balance, intelligence, and aspiration, rather than heroic action. They carried tension without action, allowed for trials to go wrong, and created self-reliance in their sons. As fathers nurture separation, sons emerge as individuals, unique and singular. Separation provides tension that is passed from one generation to the next, and at the same time the separation provides space for emergence with spiritual and earthly purpose in conjunction.

Puer and Senex

How does depth psychology explain the conflictual and distanced nature of the father/son relationship? As we have seen, Freud introduced the notion of the Oedipus complex, wherein the son becomes a rival to the father for sexual possession of the mother, and out of competition with the father, the son evolves a psychosexual identity and conscience. This relationship sets the tone for later relationship to the competitive world of work, achievement, and society in general. In particular, relationship with father imparts to the son the quality of his ability to form independent judgment, character, and tolerance of disappointment.

Eric Erickson's (1963) second stage of childhood development, autonomy versus shame, is linked to the father and located in the anal stage of development. The child is first made aware of the father principle when the primary locus of somatic concern is the back side of the body, and the primary function is one of anal control. The first impositions of authority lay the seeds for the sadomasochistic nature of the father/son relationship, but also set up the son's longing for fusion with the invisible father.[2]

In the traditional Jungian model, the father is an embodiment of the sky god, representing judgment, law and order, governance, values of civilization, ideals, tradition, collective values, religious, ethical, and social structure, authority, decisiveness, forcefulness, spirit, and sexuality. The sky father is associated with technique, logic, abstraction, and decision making. He appears in mythology and religion as the Egyptian sun god, Ra, the Hebrew god, Yahweh, the Greek gods, Zeus and Apollo, and the Norse gods, Wotan and Thor. The son, in order to achieve his own psychological identity, inner validity, and personal authority must heroically overcome the sky father and establish his own world of principles. "Father" is based on an inherited universal structure which is much more than that individual, dead or alive, back in Iowa or the Bronx. He is the image of the *principles* that form the foundation of the son's personality. It is these principles that keep abusing and swallowing the son, trying to keep out new life, values, and individual identity. Wallace Stevens gives expression to the archetypal father in his poem, *The Irish Cliffs of Moher*.

Who is my father in this world, in this house,
At the spirit's base?
My father's father, his father's father, his—
Shadows like winds
Go back to a parent before thought, before speech,
At the head of the past.
They go to the cliffs of Moher rising out of the mist,
Above the real,
Rising out of present time and place, above
The wet, green grass.
This is not landscape, full of the somnambulations
Of poetry
And the sea. This is my father or, maybe,
It is as he was,
A likeness, one of the race of fathers: earth
And sea and air.
                    (Bly, Hillman, and Meade 1992, 152)

Archetypal psychology would talk about father and son not so much in an interpretive way, but in terms of the details of the actual universal images of father and son. Father is represented by the archetype of the *senex* or "old man" embodied in the god, Saturn. Saturn is the power the son must overcome or test in order to come into his own as a man. Images of senex are old, wise man, bearded father or grandfather, judge, upholder of laws and institutions, time, scythe or sickle, rock of ages, and old tree. Senex represents the longing for a superior knowledge, institutions of learning, certainty, and the attitude of "I know."

Senex is anything that has to do with systems of order, structure, unchangeability, rigidity, fixity, intolerance, old habits, memories of times past, obsessive ruminations, coldness, remoteness, loneliness, prolonged slow rhythms, lethargy, boundaries, heaviness, leaden weight, density, depression, sickness, and death. He is the god of discipline and boundary, the god of correct failure, but also the god of sour bitterness and regret. A dream of a father indicates the appearance of senex as threat to father/son dwelling in the values of "mother earth."

I am with my son at night looking at the stars. We can see Saturn very clearly and it is relatively close compared to the other bodies in the sky. Its ring is like a huge grist mill stone turning around and around it. Saturn keeps getting closer and closer and there are rumblings of earth quakes. It seems that Saturn has gotten too close to earth and throws the planet off its course. I try to think of what will be safer, being inside or outside, but there is no safe place.

The absent or abusive father sets up a yearning for a spirit father in the son, evoking in him the archetype of *puer.* Puer means "eternal youth." Mythically, he is representative of a search for spirit in the form of the sky father and a yearning to redeem the father by surpassing him. He is constantly soaring like the mythical son, Icarus, flying toward the sun in search of the father spirit, seeking recognition from the father, but he is only able to actually experience relationship with the father as being swallowed up. Mythical images of the puer are the Egyptian god, Horus, whose absent father, Osiris, was killed and entombed before he was born and even before he was conceived. Horus as falcon soars up into the sky beyond the gods of former times, a flight representative of the search for father and the yearning to surpass the father, always destined to failure. Icarus soared toward the sun or spirit father, only to crash into the sea. Phaethon tricked his father, the sun god, into allowing him to drive his chariot across the sky, only to come falling to earth himself. Bellerophon tried to ride a flying horse to heaven but fell to earth, becoming a lonely, lame wanderer. These soaring journeys of the puer are manifested in contemporary men by leaps up the corporate ladder, sudden spurts of ascendant creativity, flashing fountains of seemingly brilliant ideas, and rebellion for its own sake. The crash to earth is representative of depressions and despair, letting it all go, inevitable failures, breakdowns, fallings apart, and the givings over of responsibility—all of which go with overly idealized ambition and are symbolized in the plane crashes of young male musicians and celebrities.

Puer, then, is the archetype of the fiery spirit in the figure of the eternal youth. He is often effeminate, taken with his own uniqueness, inspired. He shows no sign of aging, no sense of time, no patience, and no boundaries. He is one for whom fixation is death, for whom limitation presents the threat of being swallowed. He is potential, futurity, inquiry—with little completion or actual accomplishment. He is constantly searching, without roots, innocent, and untainted by grit or complexity, while oriented toward heights, spirituality, and ascendance.

The drama and interconnection of the senex/puer relationship can be seen in the modern play, *Death of a Salesman* by Arthur Miller (1949). The senex figure is Willy, age 60, husband to Linda and father of two sons, Biff and Happy. Willy is a traveling salesman, the old man as lonely, wandering goat. He did not know his own father, who left the family early in Willy's life to seek wealth in Alaska, a form of soaring leap for fortune. Willy says, "Dad left when I was such a baby and I never had a chance to talk to him and I still feel kind of temporary about myself."

Willy himself has not been present to his sons in a fundamental way, passing on masculine values of principle and practice that would enable them to make a legitimate place for themselves in the world. Instead, he has passed on to them legacies of deceit and pipedreams of exaggerated accomplishment. Willy stands by tradition and holds to the old values, but now he can no longer keep his ground. He is infirm and broken, the drive gone, as represented by his inability to make his last sales run.

Biff, the oldest son, is representative of the puer, having spent his life avoiding boundaries and wandering aimlessly. He says at one point, "I just can't take hold of some kind of life." Biff goes from job to job, yearning for the freedom of outdoor life, open sky, open spaces, and no limits. This yearning keeps him from taking hold, committing, finishing, or accomplishing. Biff says, "When spring comes to where I am, I suddenly get the feeling, my god, I'm not getting anywhere!" And then he comes "running home," like Icarus crashing to mother earth, again having failed to actualize anything of his overblown dream of buying a ranch, raising cattle, using his muscles, and living life in the great outdoors. The only way that Biff seems capable of acquiring is by stealing, an action covertly encouraged by Willy when Biff was a star athlete. Biff's only means of addressing a prospective employer is to steal the employer's golden pen, symbolic of phallic achievement and creativity.

Behind Biff's self-destructive actions is the shadow of his father's deceit and failure. Biff started out on the road to oblivion when he first learned of his father's secret affair. It is as if knowing that his father is not a man, Biff can never become a man. Through his own failure, Biff protects his father from the awareness of his own failure.

Happy, the second son, has been completely swallowed and castrated by the capitalistic values of the cultural senex. He works in a department store, unable to advance his position and perpetually resentful of his boss who he perceives as holding him down. At one point Happy exclaims, "I just want to rip my clothes off in the middle of the store and outbox that goddamned merchandise manager." Happy is caught up in the world of competition, but having no sense of his own masculine authority, can only function through stealth, taking bribes and sleeping with the fianceé of his competitor.

The play takes place in a world where relationships between fathers and sons are marked by distance, deceit, competition, castration, and engulfment. The men are basically angry and lonely, having identified with false values and having received very little that would enable them to identify with their own authority. Willy's underlying hostility toward Biff is revealed in Biff's question, "Why does dad mock me all the time? I can't reach him." Biff is drowning in Willy's dreams for him and rendered impotent by Willy's indulgence of him and his covering up for his thefts and shortcuts as a young man, not allowing him to suffer the consequences of his actions. Willy is constantly giving orders but is never able to bestow any meaningful values or masculine qualities on his sons.

In reciprocation for the fathers keeping the sons down, the sons get back at the fathers. Howard, the son of Willy's boss, fires Willy. Biff steals a golden pen from the desk of a prospective employer. Happy is constantly plotting the downfall of his own boss.

Amid this confusion of distance, deceit, and subtle violence, there is something trying to bring these lonely men, father and son, senex and puer together. Linda asks Willy, "The closer you seem to come, the more shaky he gets. The closer Biff gets, the more angry you become. Why are you so hateful to each other?" Toward the end of the play, Biff tries to hug Willy. Willy rejects him, but later becomes obsessed with planting seed in his small garden.

In the end, father and son do come together, for an instant. In the climactic scene of the play, Biff, now completely disillusioned, pleads with Willy to join with him in giving up the illusion of greatness that has nothing to do with his emerging sense of himself.

> Biff: . . . Why am I trying to become what I won't want to be? What am I doing in an office, making a contemptuous, begging fool of myself, when all I want is out there, waiting for me the minute I say I know who I am! Why can't I say that, Willy? (He tries to make Willy face him, but Willy pulls away and moves to the left.)
>
> Willy: (with hatred, threateningly) The door of your life is wide open!
>
> Biff: Pop! I'm a dime a dozen, and so are you!
>
> Willy (turning on him now in an uncontrolled outburst):   I am not a dime a dozen! I am Willy Loman, and you are Biff Loman!
>
> (Biff starts for Willy, but is blocked by Happy. In his fury, Biff seems on the verge of attacking his father.)
>
> Biff: I am not a leader of men, Willy, and neither are you. You were never anything but a hard-working drummer who landed

in the ash can like all the rest of them! I'm one dollar an hour, Willy! I tried seven states and couldn't raise it. A buck an hour! Do you gather my meaning? I'm not bringing home any prizes any more, and you're going to stop waiting for me to bring them home!

Willy: You vengeful, spiteful mut!

(Biff breaks from Happy. Willy, in fright, starts up the stairs. Biff grabs him.)

Biff: Pop, I'm nothing! I'm nothing, Pop. Can't you understand that? There's no spite in it any more. I'm just what I am, that's all.

(Biff's fury has spent itself, and he breaks down, sobbing, holding on to Willy, who dumbly fumbles for Biff's face.)

A few lines later, after Biff has left,

Willy: (After a long pause, astonished, elevated:) Isn't that— isn't that remarkable? Biff—he likes me!

In that moment of son holding father and father feeling son's face as if for the first time knowing him, the son has become a father to his father and the father has become the son. Senex and puer are merged in each of the men. But it is too late for Willy. His mind is broken now, and he has identified with the self-destructive side of the father/son archetype. Clinging to the illusion of his own and Biff's magnificence, he deliberately crashes out his life.

To conclude, the archetypal images of senex and puer tell us two things. First, father and son are two faces of the same archetype, father/son. Second, there is something of necessity in the tension, violence, and distance, as well as a yearning for each other, that occurs between the two. Fathers and sons will always be in a deathlike struggle to separate and come together. It is as if their sameness calls for conflict and division in order for their individuality to be experienced and for a reunion to occur.

Finding the Father

We have been seeing how metaphorical and literal death surrounds the relationship of father and son. There is also an experience of father for the son which is different from that of the distant, devouring sky father—namely, the earth father. In ancient Egyptian mythology, the deity of the sky is female, Nut, and the earth god is male, Geb. The Italian god, Faunus, brought fruitfulness to fields and animals. The earth father is a creative, nurturing, protecting parent, imaged as god of land, grains, streams, and animals (Colman 1993). He procreates, nurtures, and cares for his children on a continuous basis, helping to establish a basic inner trust and security. Mythically, he is the First Ancestor-Founding King, living in the underworld. This ancient forebear, fostered by the dead ancestors within the earth, was a cthonic divinity, the mediator of the vital principle that life emerges out of death, pushing up out of the soil (Perry 1966).

The image of the earth father bespeaks the softening of the senex. According to Greek mythology, old Cronus ruled a golden age on the Island of the Blessed in which men lived like gods. There was no work, no pain, and no aging, and death was like sleep. In alchemical imagery, the old king is "worked upon" through the operation of *solutio* in which the old man is soaked in a hot tub or sweat house. Like the Fisher King, he can't move, and the heat of his own sickness softens him.

Likewise, cultural history reveals that the relation between fathers and sons is not always distant or conflictual. The peoples of the ancient Near East could not have conceived of the possibility of generational conflict (Reinhold 1976, 16). In an Egyptian writing dated at 2450 B.C., Ptah-hotep gives advice to young fathers:

> If you have a household, and beget a son who pleases the god—if he does right, and inclines to your nature, and hearkens to your instructions, and his designs do good in your house, and he has regard for your substance as it befits, search out for him everything that is good. . . . A son who has heard . . . prospers after he has heard. When he has grown old and has attained honor, he talks in like manner to his children and renews the instruction of his father. (Reinhold 1976, 17–18)

Similarly, the writing of Alexis de Toqueville about American society in 1832 reveals an established order of transition between father and son.

> As soon as the young American approaches manhood, the ties of filial obedience are relaxed day by day: master of his thoughts, he is soon master of his conduct. In America, there is, strictly speaking, no adolescence: at the close of boyhood, the man appears, and begins to trace out his own path.
>
> It would be an error to suppose that this is preceded by a domestic struggle, in which the son has obtained by a sort of moral

violence the liberty that his father refused him. The same habits, the same principles, which impel the one to assert his independence, predispose the other to consider the use of that independence as an incontestable right. The former does not exhibit any of those rancorous or irregular passions which disturb men long after they have shaken off an established authority; the latter feels none of that bitter and angry regret which is apt to survive a bygone power. The father foresees the limits of his authority long beforehand, and when the time arrives, he surrenders it without a struggle: the son looks forward to the exact period at which he will be his own master; and he enters upon his freedom without precipitation and without effort, as a possession which is his own, and which no one seeks to wrest from him.

De Toqueville goes on to elaborate regarding the value structure that honors the father and the affects of democracy upon this structure.

When men live more for the remembrance of what has been than for the care of what is, and when they are more given to attend to what their ancestors thought than to think themselves, the father is the natural and necessary tie between the past and the present—the link by which the ends of these two chains are connected. In aristocracies, then, the father is not only the civil head of the family, but the organ of its traditions, the expounder of its customs, the arbiter of its manners. He is listened to with deference, he is addressed with respect, and the love which is felt for him is always tempered with fear.

When the condition of society becomes democratic, and men adopt as their general principle that it is good and lawful to judge of all things for one's self, using former points of belief not as a rule of faith, but simply as a means of information, the power which the opinions of a father exercise over those of his sons diminishes, as well as his legal power. (de Tocqueville 1956, 228–30)

Freud (1921, 1928), in addition to elucidating the conflictual dynamic between fathers and sons, emphasizes the caring and protecting aspect of the father in the early developmental stages of the son. The very young son has feelings of love and admiration for the father and forms his identity, in part, around these feelings. Psychoanalyst Hans Loewald (1951) envisioned the role of father as drawing the son out of the maternal matrix so that the son can form an active ego identification with the father as a psychosexual role model.

Native rituals around childbirth and modern infant observation reveal the strength of force in the bonding of fathers with infants. In many native tribes men go through a ritual of couvade in which the father separately experiences an imaginative child bearing at the time that the mother is delivering (Hall and Dawson 1989). Contemporary fathers, present at the birth of infants, are "elated" by the event, show strong emotional "engrossment," and begin developing a bond to the infant within three days (Greenberg and Morris 1974). On all but a few measures, fathers and mothers are equally involved in interaction with and nurturant responsiveness to the infant (Parke and Tinsley 1981). Father is recognized as such by the infant at 4 to 5 months. Infants at 7, 8, 12, and 13 months show no preference for either parent on attachment behavior measures (Lamb 1981).[3]

James Agee portrays the experience of a boy warmly held by the world of the father in his description of a father taking his young son to a bar in his novel, *A Death in the Family.*

> They turned through the swinging doors into a blast of odor and sound. There was no music: only the density of bodies and of the smell of a market bar, of beer, whiskey and country bodies, salt and leather; no clamor, only the thick quietude of crumpled talk. . . . He looked up his father's length and watched him bend backwards tossing one off in one jolt in a lordly manner, and a moment later heard him say to the man next to him, "That's my boy"; and felt a warmth of love. Next moment he felt his father's hands under his armpits, and he was lifted, high, and seated on the bar, looking into a long row of huge bristling and bearded red faces. . . . Somewhat timidly, but feeling assured that his father was proud of him and that he was liked, and liked these men, he smiled . . . and suddenly many of the men laughed. He was disconcerted by their laughter and lost his smile a moment; then realizing it was friendly, smiled again; and again they laughed. His father smiled at him. "That's my boy", he said warmly. "Six years old, and he can already read like I couldn't read when I was twice his age." (Agee 1959, 23–24)

The image of the earth father and the accounts of relatively smooth transition from boyhood to manhood through prescribed rituals, behavior patterns, and the ready relinquishing of authority by the father, infant observation, and personal accounts of childhood serve as background for the presentation of mythological images of sons joining with fathers, the puer and senex fulfilling their yearning for each other.

In Navajo mythology two hero brothers are born to Changing Woman; their father, unknown to them, is the sun god. At the age of 12, the two boys leave to find their father, going through many ordeals which Joseph Campbell (1949) calls "The Road of Trials." They must pass through rocks that crush together, reeds that cut, cactus plants that tear to pieces, sands that bury, and a river covered with water bugs. In all of these dangerous situations, they are helped by a feather, given them by a goddess, Spider Woman, which magically connects them to their father. Finally they arrive at their father's house and are hidden by his daughter. When he discovers them, he gives them three more tests of survival: a superheated sweat house, poisoned corn meal, and a fall onto sharp sticks. The sun god then recognizes them as his sons and gives them their names as well as sacred objects and wisdom to protect themselves in their adventures on earth. Campbell calls this psychological theme "Atonement With the Father," the search for the distant father through confrontation with death, resulting in the meeting with and recognition by the father from whom attributes of power are received.

The Homeric epic, *The Odyssey,* contains a progression of images of father/son renewal. Odysseus, as warrior-king and father, leaves his wife and child to fight in the Trojan War for several years and after the war, suffers years of travail and wandering in his attempt to return home. Finally, Odysseus returns to his homeland and comes first to his loyal swineherd's hut in disguise as a beggar. While he is there, Odysseus's son, Telemachos, arrives and is greeted by the old swineherd,

> as a father, with heart full of love, welcomes his only
> and grown son, for whose sake he has undergone many hardships
> when he comes back in the tenth year from a distant country.
> (*Od.* Bk XVI, 17–19)

This greeting sets up the revealing of the long-lost Odysseus to his son. Athene transforms Odysseus from the aspect of a beggar to that of himself. He then goes to Telemachos, who thinks he might be a god. Odysseus answers,

> "I am your father, for whose sake you are always grieving
> as you look for violence from others, and endure hardships."
> So he spoke, and kissed his son, and the tears running
> down his cheeks splashed on the ground.
> (*Od.* Bk. XVI, 188–91)

Telemachos is still unbelieving, and Odysseus says,

> "Telemachos, it does not become you to wonder too much
> at your own father when he is here, nor doubt him. No other
> Odysseus than I will ever come back to you. But here I am, and I
>   am as you see me, and after hardships and suffering
> much I have come, in the twentieth year, back to my own country."
> ... Now Telemachos
> folded his great father in his arms and lamented,
> shedding tears, and desire for mourning rose in both of them;
> and they cried shrill in a pulsing voice.

(Od. Bk XVI, 188–219)

Together, father and son now plot and overthrow the false suitors of the queen, Penelope. Side by side they do battle, enabling Telemachos to realize his own power as a man.

Odysseus then reveals himself to his own father, Laertes. At first, he disguises himself from his father and tells a story about himself to Laertes who

> caught up the grimy dust and poured it
> over his face and grizzled head, groaning incessantly.
> The spirit rose up in Odysseus, and now in his nostrils
> there was a shock of bitter force as he looked on his father.
> He sprang to him and embraced and kissed and then said to him:
> "Father, I am he, the man whom you ask about. I am
> here, come back in the twentieth year to the land of my father."

(Od. Bk XXIV, 316–22)

Laertes is still disbelieving, until Odysseus gives him unmistakable indication of his true identity.

> Laertes' knees and the heart within him went slack,
> as he recognized the clear proofs that Odysseus had given.
> He threw his arms around his dear son, and much enduring
> great Odysseus held him close.

(Od. Bk XXIV, 345–48)

In these scenes of painful reunion, senex and puer are connected, not only in the joining of Odysseus with his son and then with his father, but within the figure of Odysseus himself, at once father and son.

Vergil's *Aeneid* displays another image of father and son together in that of Aeneas, great Trojan leader, with his son, Iulus, and his father,

Anchises, among the ruins of their lost city. Troy is in flames, and Aeneas is ready to retreat with his family.

> "Then come, my dear father, let them place you upon my back.
> I shall carry you on my shoulders: your weight is not heavy.
> Wherever our chance may fall, one common danger,
> One safety shall be our own. . . .
> So speaking I bent my neck and on wide shoulders
> I laid a tawny lion's skin for garment
> And then took up my load. Little Iulus
> Entwined his fingers in my right hand and followed
> His father with steps not equal, my wife behind us.
> We walked through shadows.
>
> (*An.* II, 741–66)

So Aeneas shoulders his father, as all sons must take on the influence of their father, and guides his son through the "shadows," three generations retreating from the ruins of the past to found a new homeland.

After Anchises has died, Aeneus visits his soul in the underworld, and Anchises bestows upon Aeneas wisdom in the form of knowledge of his origins and his future. We find Anchises in the underworld looking longingly over the souls of the dead for his descendants.

> Father Anchises, deep in a blooming valley,
> Examined quite closely those souls which would rise to the light,
> Reviewing by chance the number of all his descendants,
> The grandsons so dear, their fates and fortunes and deeds,
> Their characters too. When he saw Aeneas approaching
> Toward him through the grass, he stretched eager hands toward
>   his son,
> His cheeks bathed with tears, and managed to utter this word:
> "You have come at last, that loyalty which I knew
> Has conquered your difficult course. Do I really see
> Your face, son of mine? Do I hear and reply to your words?
> So I felt in my heart that I should, and I reckoned the hours
> Before you could come: anxiety did not deceive me.
> What lands and wide seas you have travelled to reach me, my
>   son,
> And beset by what dangers! How I feared that the powers of
>   Libya

Might injure you!" Aeneas spoke: "It was your sad image
Appearing again and again that brought me, my father, to this
   threshold."

(An. Bk VI, 687–703)

Anchises reveals and passes on to Aeneus his rightful inheritance, the
mysteries: the ways of the underworld, the reincarnation of soul into body,
the glory that is to come for his race when it resettles finally in Rome, and
the ideals that are to be the foundations for that future culture. These mysteries, knowledge of past and future, and the ways of life on all levels of being
are the ultimate boon that a father can bestow upon his son.

In Navajo, Greek, and Roman mythology we have different images of
fathers and sons from those of swallowing, castration, deceit, and violent revolt
that make up one part of this configuration. Here the two faces of the archetype
blend as one into images of rescuing, holding, mutuality, planning, working,
and fighting together, and giving and receiving of knowledge of life's mysteries.

Who is the god who mediates the exchange of hostility and love
between father and son, creating the permeability that allows for the connection between the two? It is Hermes/Mercury, the dual-natured god of
liminal states and paradoxes who is, at once, senex and puer. Alchemical
depictions of fathers and sons show Mercurius between the two, bringing
father and son together. The tie between fathers and sons will always be
mercurial, never straight, with flittings back and forth, painful distancing
and conflict here and warm togetherness there.

The father recognizes the son and the son recognizes the father. The
father is honored for the attributes he brings, and he gives them freely—
knowledge, discriminating action, and identity. They are the gifts, as Robert
Bly writes, of

> a black overcoat around the soul, invisible in our black nights. He
> gave, and gives a sheathing, or envelope, or coating around the
> soul made of intensity, shrewdness, desire to penetrate, liveliness,
> impulse, daring. The father's birth gift cannot be quantified. His
> gift contributes to the love of knowledge, love of action and ways
> to honor the world of things. (Bly 1990, 121)

Hamlet and Oedipus: The Failed Father and Memory

The questions that persist for the son—who is my father? where is my father?
can I trust my father?—are questions of discovery for sons, simultaneous

discovery of self and world, and discovery of the fact that the self/world interface allows for a unique, individual quality of experience. In India there is a story of a father who takes his baby to the mountaintop and says, "This is the world. I will introduce you." A Mayan Indian saying states that father must take baby to the highest hill so that he can see his world.

One way that sons are brought into the world is through achieving retribution or revenge for the father. A myth from the Hittite culture of 1400–1200 B.C., in what is now Turkey, tells of Alalu, the first god, who ruled for nine years. He is dethroned by Anu, god of heaven, who also rules for nine years. Anu, in turn, is besieged by Alalu's son, Kumarbi.

> Kumarbi, Alalu's offspring, gave battle against Anu.
> Anu no longer withstood Kumarbi's eyes;
> he slipped out of his hands and fled, Anu (did),
> and went up to the sky.
> After him Kumarbi rushed
> and seized him, Anu, by his feet
> and pulled him down from the sky.
> He bit his loins
> (so that) his manhood united with Kumarbi's interior like bronze.
> When it united,
> when Kumarbi swallowed Anu's manhood,
> he rejoiced and laughed.
>
> (Kramer 1961, 156–57)

William Shakespeare's play, *Hamlet*, depicts among many themes, the struggle of sons to come to terms with father through revenge. The play starts with the revelation that the younger Fortinbras is now seeking to retake the lands his father lost to Hamlet's father years before. The ghost of Hamlet's father then calls upon his mourning son to revenge his death. The new king, Claudius, bids Hamlet to forget his dead father and "think of us as a father" (I, ii, ll 107–8). Polonius, the Lord Chamberlain, reveals himself as a foolish father—burdening his son Laertes with truisms and false wisdom upon Laertes' departure. When Hamlet kills Polonius, Laertes becomes another foil to Hamlet and seeks to revenge his father. He plots with Claudius to kill Hamlet. In the fight that ensues, fathers and sons kill each other off and a new son, Fortinbras, establishes a new kingdom.

In *Hamlet*, fathers fail; they can't hold power—Old Fortinbras loses his land, Hamlet's father loses his kingdom, Polonius loses respect, Claudius loses his scheme—and sons struggle with the failure of the father. James

Hillman (1987a) notes that failure is inherent to fathers, but it is precisely the father's failings that father the son and bring him into the world. In the Greek myth of Oedipus, Oedipus's struggle to know himself by realizing who his father was, is the struggle to meet and embrace fate, character, destiny. When Oedipus comes to know himself, through the knowledge that he killed his father, he blinds himself, indicating his newly found identity is unified with "in-sight," psychological seeing or imaginative reflection, and wanders the world as his home. In the final play that Sophocles wrote in the Oedipus trilogy, *Oedipus at Colonus,* old Oedipus, now fathered by time, having cursed his own sons to death, comes to a new son, Theseus, looking for a place to die. Oedipus presents himself as failed: "I come to give you something, and the gift, / Is my own beaten self" (ll. 576–77).

Fathers fail—Hamlet's father comes as tormented spirit, and Odysseus arrives as beggar—and sons like Aeneas and Odysseus or Kumarbi and Hamlet rescue and revenge fathers. A man in his younger 30s who struggled with a dominating father dreams:

> A ceremonial event happens and it is like I am reading my own account of the incident in an old newspaper or magazine. It is to commemorate the fall of antiquity. The earth trembles, wild animals and natives are out, and it is dangerous to be away from cover. I am near an old Greek ceremonial ground. Statues and relics are crashing. These are only substitutes of some sort, though, and the genuine articles will be maintained.
>
> A giant symbolic wheel of stone is dislodged and rolls across the ceremonial grounds. My father, in a foolish, child-like impulse, runs out to throw a stick at the rolling wheel as if to stop it. A strong-muscled, black, native chieftain, with a white sheet draped around him, runs up behind my father and throws a spear at his back. It is clear that the spear will hit its mark either killing or seriously wounding Dad. It is clear also that I am supposed to go out on a horse to pick him up and take him away. All of this is part of the ceremony.

The father-world, childlike and impotent in the dreamer's father, tries to stop the wheel of fate and the son's individuation. The spirit of the warrior-king refuses to let this happen, and it is part of the young man's initiation into manhood and the world to redeem the spirit of the fallen father by carrying it himself.

What do fathers want? They want memory. With the guidance of Hermes, Priam crosses the battle lines in the middle of the night to beg for the body of his dead son so that he can bury it, placing his son in memorium. Anchises, Achilles, and Agamemnon all wait in the underworld for sight or news of their sons to feed their souls. The ghost of Hamlet's father tells him, "Remember me" (I, v, 91), echoing the words of old Oedipus near his death, "Remember me, / Be mindful of my death" (ll. 1553–54). The old man longs to remember and to be remembered. Robert Bly:

> This body offers to carry us for nothing—as the ocean carries logs—so on some days the body wails with its great energy, it smashes up the boulders, lifting small crabs, that flow around the sides. Someone knocks on the door, we do not have time to dress. He wants us to come with him through the blowing and rainy streets, to the dark house. We will go there, the body says, and there find the father whom we have never met, who wandered in a snowstorm the night we were born, who then lost his memory, and has lived since longing for his child, whom he saw only once . . . while he worked as a shoemaker, as a cattle herder in Australia, as a restaurant cook who painted at night. When you light the lamp you will see him. He sits there behind the door . . . the eyebrows so heavy, the forehead so light . . . lonely in his whole body, waiting for you. (Bly 1986b, 132)

CHAPTER SIX

The Torture of Relationship/
The Rites of Marriage

First of all there came Chaos
and after him came
Gaia of the broad breast
. . . and Tartaros the foggy in the pit
of the wide-wayed earth,
and Eros, who is love, handsomest among all
the immortals,
who breaks the limbs' strength,
who in all gods, in all human beings
overpowers the intelligence in the breast,
and all their shrewd planning.

        —Hesiod, *Theogony*

Love, Deceit, Fear, Labour, Envy, Fate, Old Age, Death,
Darkness, Misery, Lamentation, Favour, Fraud, Obstinacy,
the Destinies, the Hesperidies, and Dreams; all which are
the offspring of Erebus and Night.

        —Cicero, *Of the Nature of the Gods*

The Forging of the "Third"

"Relationship" is a contemporary term and a myth of our time. It is a myth
in that it is a primary organizer of the way we conduct and think about
ourselves. We tend to think that being in relationship is a panacea for our
ills, it takes care of everything. We load all of our desires onto the shoulders
of relationship—our desire for love and companionship, laughter and
conversation, intimacy and adversity, silliness and complexity, calm and
chemistry, sex and home life, romance and routine, freedom and commit-
ment. And yet when we find relationship, we often end up feeling anything

but connected and gratified. Relationship eventually brings out the craziest and the worst in us, and we see our partners in the most damning light. We can't leave it, and yet it openly or secretly feels like a kind of death, a giving up of what we hold to be our "selves."

There are many books and experts to tell us the how's of relationship—how to choose partners, how to communicate, how to work on the relationship, how to avoid projection and power conflicts, how to appreciate ourselves and our partners according to systems of personality traits, how to make it right, get what we want, make it work, and so on—all of which keep us removed from the actual experience and meaning of the relationship itself.

Relationship, in many ways, turns out to be a "fall." After getting to know who that other individual is, falling in love turns out to be a downer, a descent into Dis (Hell)—a sea of feelings of discomfort, disappointment, disconnection, disillusionment, and disintegration. Plato helps us here by connecting the initial feeling of desire and the resulting feeling of hell. Through Socrates in the *Cratylus* (403c, d), Plato tells us that Hades binds the soul through desire (*eros*), and that no desire is stronger than that of relationship.

Plato is telling us that there is something about us—*psyche,* soul, or essential being—that wants to go down. It is as if the soul paradoxically wants an experience of change that involves feelings associated with death such as loss, pain, and suffering. The soul finds a form, a relationship, to fill this need as a way of coming into its own essential nature. It is as if the suffering of relationship enabled the coming into visibility of the soul, like the suffering of childbirth is the coming into visibility of new life. To imagine this, we would see that in contemporary life we don't have civil war, but we do have its equivalent in relational strife. We have distanced ourselves from biological death, but we have divorce instead. (Over half of all marriages end in divorce.) In short, relationship serves the comtemporary soul as a container for its suffering and ensuing renewed formation.

Seeing relationship as a matter of the soul's choosing enables us to see the relationship as a living entity in itself, a third body, something that works on us. An orientation from the standpoint of relationship would be not, what can it do for me, but what does it want from us, what are its needs? Robert Bly (1986a) has written a poem about this third body shared by two, "A Man and A Woman Sit Near Each Other."

> A man and a woman sit near each other, and they do not long
> At this moment to be older, or younger, nor born
> in any other nation, or time, or place.

They are content to be where they are, talking or not-talking.
Their breaths together feed someone whom we do not know.
The man sees the way his fingers move;
he sees her hands close around a book she hands to him.
They obey a third body that they share in common.
They have made a promise to love that body.
Age may come, parting may come, death will come.
A man and a woman sit near each other;
as they breathe they feed someone we do not know, someone
we know of, whom we have never seen.

Bly's poem echoes a similar poem, "The Ecstasy," by John Donne in
which Donne writes about how love brings about the detachment of soul
from two bodies.

Our souls (which to advance their state
    Were gone out) hung 'twixt her and me.
And whilst our souls negotiate there,
    We like sepulchral statues lay.

The two souls then intertwine into one "abler soul."

But as all several souls contain
    Mixture of things, they know not what,
Love these mixed souls doth mix again,
    And makes both one, each this and that.
A single violet transplant,
    The strength, the color, and the size,
(All which before was poor and scant)
    Redoubles still, and multiplies.
When love, with one another so
    Interinanimates two souls,
That abler soul, which thence doth flow,
    Defects of loneliness controls.

(Harrison 1959, 372)

The resulting "ecstacy" of love is knowledge. "We then, who are this new
soul, know / Of what we are composed, and made." In other words, it is the
recognition and alignment with a third soul that allows for knowledge of self.

One way to think of the "third" of relationship is as the child between
two adults. Ancient Jewish tradition relates that the child about to be

conceived hovers over the couple in intercourse (Halevi 1979, 14). It is as if the future child brings the couple together as depicted in the movie *Back to the Future,* where the young man who has emerged from a time machine finds himself in the past when his future parents haven't met yet. He desperately tries to get them together so that he can have his own life. The child can also be the imaginal child shared by a couple—the abandoned child that each partner sees in the other and wants to rescue and care for (Hillman 1975a, 14–15).

The "third" might also be seen as the dialogue or script between two people. As Donne alludes, the other person brings out words, feelings, and attitudes that we need to know about ourselves. It is as if people get together when they find someone with whom they can share a script and then struggle to get on the same page. In this way, relationship becomes a matter of who can take the part of the other in the dialogue we are trying to work through. Staying or leaving becomes not so much an orientation to the other person, but staying with or leaving the dialogue. If one person leaves, who will come through with the setup lines or the punch lines? Who will bring out my hidden anger or my pressing need to feel responsible?

Alchemical Coupling

We are considering the idea of relationship as an encompassing third body, something that holds and works upon two people, and we are focusing our attention on the experience of suffering involved in this process. For many centuries, up through the Renaissance, the practitioners of alchemy (a combination of chemical science and speculative philosophy) attempted to describe the process of change as part of the work of nature. Alchemy came to provide many images for changes in nature, including painful aspects of life that are difficult for the modern age to see as a "natural." These images can serve as metaphors for different facets of relationship.

The *prima materia* was the name given to the "first matter," the gross ore at the beginning of the process that needed refining, which serves as a metaphor for the situation within and between individuals at the start. Aristotle called the *prima materia* simply something that isn't there yet. In relationship this could refer to the initial encounter with the stranger across the crowded room, at the Halloween party, or in the class. More to the point, the *prima materia* is the latent condition of the soul that needs to be brought forward. I may be sensitive and nurturing, but I may also be secretly angry and need to have that anger brought out through relationship. I may be very good at taking responsibility, but I also need to be able to be taken care of. Relationship serves as my means for working through this conflict.

The *prima materia* was called the *increatum,* meaning the unformed, that undeveloped mass in us that needs to be given form through the pressures and stresses provided by relationship. It is ubiquitous; it shows up everywhere, so that it doesn't matter if we are on vacation or at the dinner table—the same dynamic will occur. As the initial attraction wears away, the underlying revulsion becomes more visible. We don't want to see this vulgarity of which we are a part, and people in relationship do lots of different things to keep from getting close to each other to avoid feeling pain.

There were many disturbing names for the *prima materia* including the "vile face" and "the orphan," but also the "Redeemer." What is most repulsive is that which ultimately can change us. We are bound to get together with just that person who is most likely to annoy us, imitate our sense of self, or become our worst nightmare. "The milk of the virgin" refers to our innocent, naive nature that needs to be darkened by the rape that comes with relationship. The "hidden fire" is the desire that has been kept secret, perhaps from fear of disappointment, that constant burning that says, "all I need is to find the right lover." "The infinite" are the big, airy questions in life, wherein relationships form around causes and global attitudes that need to be grounded. The "red earth" is the animal, earthy nature that attracts people with predominately abstract qualities.

In summary, relationship provides a container where the work that is necessary to change a predominant condition, attitude, or quality—the *prima materia*—in the individual personality can take place, and this work is often painful.

The work or *opus* of alchemy consisted of many kinds of operations that were performed upon the *prima materia.* Practitioners called it "torturing" the material. It is like cooking, where there are many different means of preparing the raw food—frying, deep frying, baking, boiling, double-boiling, broiling, simmering, cooling off, letting it sit, or diluting, and the alchemists worked from similar recipes or formulas.

One of the major alchemical operations, *calcinatio,* had to do with fire and heating. The fire in relationship is the fire of desire, sexual desire and love, but also the fire of frustration and rage when it doesn't go the way we want. *Calcinatio,* in its destructive form, flares up in domestic violence. People may be attracted to relationships in which they become angry or experience their own anger through the anger of another. They may be attracted to relationships that provide mostly frustration. The result of the anger and frustration, however, may be to burn off or dry out old waterlogged feelings of remorse and self-pity or old ways of hiding in the brush. A man who had been through a short but volatile relationship that ended explosively, dreamed that he had become sheriff of a small town located between where he lived and where his former girlfriend lived. In the dream the former sheriff had been something of a misfit. In the town there is a space that had been an open furnace or smelting pit. Now some men are sitting around a small fire in this pit, talking and telling stories of the way things were. The dream depicts an atmosphere in which there has been an intense heat that has contributed to the "burnout" of a misfit quality in the dreamer that needed to be refined or changed in order for there to be a fresh start.

Fire is also the fire of the Greek god, Hephaistos, forging the creations of the world. The heat of friction between partners creates new ways of seeing life. An alchemical recipe reads as follows:

> Take a fierce gray wolf, which . . . is found in the valleys and mountains of the world, where he roams almost savage with hunger. Cast to him the body of the King, and when he has devoured it, burn him entirely to ashes in a great fire. By this process the King will be liberated. (Edinger 1985, 18)

The hungry wolf is that part of us that is insatiable with desire for something, but we can't let it get near for fear it will devour us. The king is what we think we are, the way things should be. Metaphorically, we might say the hunger *for* relationship devours this old way of being, and is, in turn, devoured by the continual burning *of* relationship. From this burning a new king emerges, a new way of being.

Coagulatio is the alchemical process of coming together, being made into flesh, "getting real." We coagulate through encorporation, and eating together is one of the most important rituals of relationship. Eros in many ways is organized around oral needs, and the table is important as the first place of intimacy. Dinner, wine, and conversation is the place where intimacy is born.

Another metaphor for relationship has to do with water. The alchemists called the operation with water *solutio*. We talk about "diving in," "getting our feet wet," or getting "swept away" in relation to another person. There is something about the all-encompassing nature of relationship that is like a tub, fountain, pool, or wave of water that gives promise of dissolving that which is rigid, fixed, and static. The tears that come within relationship speak of the experience of feeling that cleans out a situation.

A common alchemical combination of operations was "dissolve and coagulate." The entire process was seen as one of continuous dissolving and coming together. We come together, or "get it together," through relationship. We become focused, grounded, and embodied through our intimate dealings with another individual. Often this feels like being fixed, trapped, and imprisoned because the spirit in us always wants the freedom of possibility away from the constraints of the other. The relationship then turns to a watery form, dissolving itself in preparation for the next reunification.

A parable from alchemy (Silberer 1970) describes a lonely wanderer who comes across a newly wed prince and princess in a garden. The protagonist makes the startling statement that the maid, who was supposed to be the mother of the bridegroom, was still so young that she appeared to be just born, while at the same time, sister to the groom. The maid is mother, newborn, and sister all at once! In relationship, each party becomes parent, lover, and child, nurturing and merging, while at the same time the relationship itself parents both parties as siblings.

The bride and groom are trapped in a chamber, as if their marriage were a kind of prison. The protagonist builds a small fire to keep them warm. This gently continuous fire is called the "love fire" by the alchemists, that vigilant attention and care paid to the process. The princess starts weeping; her tears continue until they flood the couple, and the two drown. The fire maintained by the protagonist keeps the water warm, it evaporates and forms clouds, which produce rain, and the cycle occurs all over again. The process of drenching and drying recurs over and over until bridegroom and bride lay, dead, rotten, and hideously stinking before the eyes of the storyteller. Then the cycle changes so that the clouds, instead of raining, condense into dew, providing a kind of moistening to the bodies, a cleansing so that the bodies become white again and eventually come back to life.

We can see from this parable that the recurring cycle of despair and drying out that is often experienced through relationship had an intention—the blackening or death of the old bodies or the way of being that no longer served its purpose. This blackened state of helplessness and hopelessness which we call depression or despair, then gave rise to a gentler process involving moistening instead of drowning. The result of the moistening was a kind of baptism or anointment of a new body, a third life, the relationship itself which encompassed the two individual partners.

The "Frog King" (Campbell 1972) is another tale of the torture of relationship as the bringing together of disparate elements like fire and water, which work upon each other until joined into a third form. In the initial situation there are two dissimilar realms next to each other, that of a princess and that of a frog. The princess's world is high and dry, filled with bright light, beauty, perfection, and solar energy. The adjacent realm is that of the frog—a forest, dark and dank, with a well that drops into the depths. In terms of conventional logic, the two realms exclude each other (bright-dark, dry-wet, beautiful-ugly, sun-moon), but the tale tells of their need for each other.

The princess plays by herself; she is unrelated in her perfection. One day she is playing with her golden ball when it goes off course as if on its own volition, evades her hands, and rolls into the well. The golden ball of perfection, her soul, has fallen into the dark realm of imperfection as if it needed something down there. The princess is distraught and weeps bitterly— already a change is happening as the wetness of feeling has been brought into her dry world. The frog retrieves the ball on condition that the princess love him. She consents but then goes back on her word once she has the ball. She turns her back on the frog and goes back up to her castle.

The princess embodies the ideals of all we think we want to be, while the frog is all that we despise—the disgusting and slimy, what we don't like about ourselves and the world, all that is repugnant, what we regret, don't admit, have forgotten, devalued. The frog wants the princess to accept him, but she can't abide him. After she leaves, he pursues her up the stairs of her castle. The frog has now crossed the boundary and gone from "down below" to "up above." He has brought his darkness, wetness, ugliness, and loathsome quality into the realm of dryness, light, and beauty.

The princess again refuses him, but the king, her father, insisting that she stay with her fate, asks the important question, "What does the frog want with you?" When we ask, "What does *it* want?" we are coming nearer to addressing the life of the relationship itself.

The frog is invited to table. The table is the place of encorporation and embodiment, the first place of transformation. Taking food with another is taking in the other. The princess is still resistant, she can't stomach the frog. The king again insists that the process be maintained, and the princess next takes the frog to her bedroom. She again refuses to take him in and as he persists, something unexpected happens. The princess becomes like the frog and instinctively throws the frog against the wall. The froglike aspect of the princess is brought out from hiding. At this point the princelike aspect of the frog can also emerge. The frog turns into a prince, and they marry.

The golden ball falls and the king holds to the process with the ultimate result that the princess becomes froglike, the frog becomes like the princess, and the two worlds come together, forming an encompassing third realm.

Falling in love is falling into the whole story—castle and forest, bedroom and well, fire and water alike—which brings about a torturous transformation for both parties. Exactly what we dislike most in our partner is what secretly attracts us, because it is that quality which then works on the hidden part of us. For all of the suffering that each partner in relationship, as princess and frog, feels at the hands of the other, the result is change into a more particular, unique form of being.

Alchemy views death, not as a final ending, nor as a short reprieve before a glowing and triumphant rebirth. In alchemy death is a goal, a condition to be sought after early in the work that enables the emergence of further changes in the overall cycle. Alchemists called death *nigredo,* a condition we think of as depression, "in the dumps," "in the pits," "stuck," or "helpless and hopeless." Alchemically, death comes as a form of decay, putrifaction, decomposition, as well as a crucifixion, rending apart, or dismembering. One alchemist, Paracelsus, said that the work of transformation proceeds from one death to another. From this idea, we might say that what marks relationship as psychological event are the death experiences—a series of relationships moving from one death to another, or within any one relationship the movement from death to death with each blow up, argument, or falling out.

Alchemy is careful to delineate *what* dies in any one body. When we feel despair, we think, "I" am depressed. In alchemy, it is only one aspect in the whole that dies. It may be that our hopes for creativity are planted in bad soil, our sulphurous, manic need to keep busy has run its course, or our naive, airy ambitions yearn for the salt of the earth—and these hopes, manias, and ambitions need to die. In alchemy it is the metal that is being worked upon that dies; *it* has a life of its own that needs to come to an end so that another metal, an amalgam, can be formed. Jung says about the "it" that experiences death:

> it is not the adept (person) who suffers all this, rather *it* suffers in him, *it* is tortured, *it* passes through death and rises again. All this happens, not to the alchemist himself but to the true man, whom he feels is near him and in him and at the same time in the (cooking vessel). (Jung 1970, 349)

James Hillman (1982b) has pointed us to a section written by D. H. Lawrence in his novel, *The Rainbow,* which graphically illustrates the impersonal connections of relationship. Lawrence is writing about a couple, a restless young woman, Ursula, and a young soldier, Skrebensky. The connection between them is not so much of man to woman but the tension between two living materials, salt and iron. Skrebensky, as iron, creates a "deadness" around Ursula, as salt, when they attend wedding festivities. She finds relief only in the passion of the dark night air. As the two dance, their wills lock, "never fusing, never yielding one to the other," a "contest in flux" (Lawrence 1961, 316). Ursula, as salt, receives the energy of the moon, symbolically associated with salt (Jung 1970), while at the same time, she feels the dark impure magnetism, the dross, of Skrebensky.

In a setting symbolically associated with the irrational—the stockyard, the moon, the night, the corn stacks—Skrebensky somehow knows in himself that he will die. He tries to capture her "brilliant, cold, salt-burning body in the soft iron of his own hands," but can't. "She took him in the kiss, hard her kiss seized upon him, hard and fierce and burning corrosive as the moonlight . . . Till gradually his warm, soft iron yielded, yielded and she was there fierce, corrosive, seething with his destruction, seething like some cruel corrosive salt around the last substance of his being, destroying him, destroying him in the kiss." Skrebensky "was not any more," he was "nothingness" (Lawrence 1961, 320).

The conflict is not between a man and a woman, two individual people, but two qualities, imagined as the minerals salt and iron, housed in two personalities. It is not the person, Skrebensky, who dies, but the quality of iron around which he has organized his personality. John Donne wrote in his poem, "The Canonization,"

> Call us what you will, we are made such by love;
> Call her one, me another fly,
> We're tapers too, and at our own cost die,
> And we in us find th' eagle and the dove.
> The Phoenix riddle hath more wit
> By us; we two being one, are it.
> So to one neutral thing both sexes fit,
> We die and rise the same, and prove
> Mysterious by this love.
>
> (Harrison 1959, 366)

Love consumes the couple, as fire does a candle, but both rise together in a mysterious "neutral thing." Ursula and Skrebensky "fit" in the way that a couple often does, with an aspect of one "killing" an aspect in the other, which in turn, creates an encompassing amalgam or unique form like the "phoenix." In relationship we secretly choose that person who has the qualities to torture or "cook" us so that we become what we need to be in alignment with the relationship becoming what it needs to be.

The Mythical Couple

Ivan Ilyich, the radical critic of culture, has suggested that marriage was invented by the church in the Middle Ages as a way of asserting control over the private lives of the peasants. In fact, marriage has been a sacred ritual since well before the advent of Christianity. Marriage is associated with comedy which classically ends with a wedding as a form of fertility ritual in which Hymen, the god of marriage, appears and sings his songs. Traditionally, the wedding as fertility rite brings in the New Year Comedy celebrating new life, as opposed to tragedy, which is a celebration of death—death of the old king, death of the old year. In this section, I explore the ancient mythical and ritual background to marriage, and to its archetypal significance as a rite of both fertility and death at once.

The ancient Babylonian ritual of marriage is based on the myth of Inanna, goddess of life and death, of fertility and famine, storehouse and slaughterhouse. She is the awakening force, stirring love in humans, ripeness in plants, and fecundity in animals. She is also the power of war, destruction, and death. The ancient poetess Enheduanna wrote of Inanna that she was "lady of all essences." She was "clothed in radiance," but at the same time, "like a dragon (she) filled the land with venom. . . . (she was) a flood descending . . . (and her) fire (blew) about and (dropped) on our nation" (Qualls 1988, 31).

Already we have a connection we aren't used to: love associated with death. Love brings out the creative potential in us, but creativity is a form of death to old ways. Death, in turn, gives the ground for new life. These two conditions reflect the two central aspects of marriage: fertility and underworldly being. Marriage is a mode of experiencing the underworld as well as a mode of generativity. The darkness of the underworld provides depth to the wellsprings of creativity.

The myth of Inanna tells the story of her marriage to a young vegetation god, Dumuzi. In imitation of this marriage, Bablylonian kings competed for the favor of the goddess. Every year a sacred marriage rite took place wherein a vegetation god would marry the goddess. A sacred prostitute acted in the stead of the goddess; the king served in the stead of the young vegetation god. The marriage was a time of festivity and religious celebration in the community, and every marriage that took place received its validity as a reenactment of the communal event which, in turn, took its validity from the mythological event. In marriage, there is a direct connection between the divine and the mortal—the human experiences the happening of the gods, and the gods are made human.

Preparation Rites

The first section of the myth of Inanna has to do with the establishment of the Garden of Paradise around the "tree of life," which stands as the foundation for every marriage. Each marriage is the creation of a new world. The tree of life is the pillar and symbolic center of the world. Its leaves extend to the heavens, its trunk sets off the earth, and its roots descend into the underworld. From the tree come the central images linking public and private life, the throne and the marriage bed, which constantly reflect each other during the marriage rite.

Inanna plucks the tree from the river and plants it in her garden, representing marriage as a civilizing event. Bringing the tree from the untamed realm into the garden is the taming of instinct and the formation of culture that is a part of every marriage. One of the original Greek meanings for the word "to marry" is "to tame." Through marriage the individual enters into identity, stepping into history by fixing the flux of time. When we publicly say "I do," we are also saying "I am."

> Inanna cared for the tree with her hand.
> She settled the earth around the tree with her foot.
> she wondered:
>> "How long will it be until I have a shining throne to sit upon?
>> How long will it be until I have a shining bed to lie upon?"[1]

The hero, Gilgamesh, drives out the Anzu-bird, the serpent, and the sorceress Lilith, all symbolic of instinct, and fashions a throne and a marriage bed for Inanna.

Inanna goes to the sheepfold, leans against the apple tree, and delights in her vulva: "Rejoicing at her wondrous vulva, the young woman Inanna applauded herself," unselfconsciously celebrating her experience of pleasure and power of generation.

Inanna then travels across the waters and visits her grandfather, Enki, god of wisdom. The two drink together, and the intoxicated Enki bestows his gifts upon Inanna. She receives powers in every realm of life—priesthood, godship, shepherdship, truth, underworld, dagger and sword, loosening and binding of hair, the art of lovemaking and of war, musical ability, song, heroism, treachery, lamentations, rejoicing, travel, dwelling-place, craft, perception, fire, the weary arm, kindling of strife, and decisions.

The imaginal dissolving of incest boundaries between father and daughter in which father acknowledges his daughter's sexuality is vital for her womanhood. Through this acknowledgment, he bestows upon her the ability to "rule her kingdom" in the world with all of the knowledge and power to which she has a rightful claim. Women who do not receive this acknowledgment are wounded and become destined to attempt to receive it from the world in self-destructive ways.

Sacred Marriage

Courtship is an important part of the rites of marriage. Inanna is wooed by the farmer and the shepherd. The tender of the flock, Dumuzi, wins out, but Inanna still resists, creating conflict which heats up the passion of the lovers. Dumuzi finally triumphs by comparing himself to her brother ("I am as good as Utu"), and her mother proclaims that he will be both father and mother to Inanna. In marriage, one partner takes on the guise of all the members of the other's family.

> Inanna, at her mother's command,
> Bathed and anointed herself with scented oil.
> She covered her body with the royal white robe.
> She readied her dowry.
> She arranged her precious lapis beads around her neck.
> She took her seal in her hand.

Making up one's face, preparing one's body, putting one's attributes in order—all are representative of aligning one's private world to the order of the cosmos.

When the lovers finally meet alone, it is a secret rendezvous, indicating the necessity of stealth for lovers. They intermingle their energies, like Shiva and Shakti, the great divine lovers of Hindu religion, immersing themselves in each other's energies.

> Dumuzi looked at her joyously.
> He pressed his neck close against hers.
> He kissed her.
> Inanna spoke:
>   "What I tell you
>   Let the singer weave into song . . .
>   My vulva, the horn,
>   The Boat of Heaven,
>   Is full of eagerness like the young moon.
>   My untilled land lies fallow . . ."

Dumuzi replied:
> "Great Lady, the king will plow your vulva.
> I, Dumuzi the King, will plow your vulva."
... Inanna sang:
> "My honey-man, my honey-man sweetens me always.
> My lord, the honey-man of the gods,
> He is the one my womb loves best.
> His hand is honey, his foot is honey,
> He sweetens me always. . . ."
Dumuzi sang:
> "O Lady, your breast is your field.
> Inanna, your breast is your field.
> Your broad field pours out plants. . . .
> Water flows from on high for your servant. . . .
> Pour it out for me, Inanna.
> I will drink all you offer."

Each becomes the world for the other, they live only for each other in eternal embrace. As they intertwine privately, the public world is made productive—the field is plowed, plants sprout, waters flow.

> She called for it, she called for it, she called for the bed!
> ... "Let the bed that rejoices the heart be prepared!
> ... Let the bed of kingship be prepared!
> Let the bed of queenship be prepared!"
> ... He put his hand in her hand.
> He put his hand to her heart.
> Sweet is the sleep of hand-to-hand.
> Sweeter still the sleep of heart-to-heart.

The marriage bed is established as the center of the couple's world, corresponding to the symbolic "world tree" as world axis. Wendel Berry (1977) notes that when Odysseus returns home, Penelope tests him by ordering the marriage bed be made up outside the bedroom. When Odysseus hears this, he becomes angry, and Penelope knows beyond a doubt that he is her true husband. Odysseus had built the bedroom around an old olive tree and had shaped the trunk into a bedpost for the marriage bed so that it could never be moved. The order of the marriage is centered in the bed which we will now see is paralleled by the centering of kingdom in the throne.

The Sacred Marriage takes place between Inanna and her king. In the marriage proclamation there is a movement back and forth between the private and public realms, the blessing of each reflecting the other. The queen announces publicly that Dumuzi has "smoothed my black boat with cream" and "quickened my narrow boat with milk," allowing for the land to be fertile and enabling Dumuzi to take the throne as king.

Ninshubur, the faithful servant of the holy shrine of Uruk,
Led Dumuzi to the sweet thighs of Inanna and spoke:
   "My queen, here is the choice of your heart,
   The king, your beloved bridegroom.
   May he spend long days in the sweetness of your holy loins.
   Give him a favorable and glorious reign.
   Grant him the king's throne, firm in its foundations.
   Grant him the shepherd's staff of judgment.
   Grant him the enduring crown with the radiant and noble
diadem.
   . . . Under his reign let there be vegetation,
   Under his reign let there be rich grain.
   . . . May the Lady of Vegetation pile the grain in heaps and
mounds.

The wedding celebrates and makes fruitful both couple and community, each reflecting the other. Berry writes:

It is possible to imagine a marriage bond that would bind a woman and a man not only to each other, but to the community of marriage, the amorous communion at which all couples sit: the sexual feast and celebration that joins them to all living things and to the fertility of the earth, and the sexual responsibility that joins them to the human past and the human future. (Berry 1977, 120)

Marriage and Death

In Euripides' play, *Iphigenia in Aulis,* Iphegenia readies herself for her wedding, which she thinks will be to a Greek hero. The great irony that runs throughout the play is that her marriage is to death. In fact, she is going to be executed, and her wedding ceremony is to be a sacrificial rite with herself as the victim.
   We usually think of marriage only as a celebration of well being, fulfillment, and prosperity, but it is also an ironic form of sacrificial death.

Adolph Guggenbuhl-Craig refers to marriage as a sacrifice for the sake of salvation, that is, for the sake of achieving a "wholeness" that is greater than what we know of ourselves.

> The tenacity of marriage as an institution, the fact that it continues to be popular despite its pain-inflicting structure, becomes easier to understand if we turn our attention to images that have nothing to do with well-being.
> The central issue in marriage is not well-being or happiness; it is . . . salvation. (Guggenbuhl-Craig 1977, 124)

> The quest for salvation, has to do not only with becoming whole; it also demands renunciatory sacrifice. Something must be given away or given up, or to put it paradoxically: to the process of achieving wholeness belongs the sacrifice, the actual renunciation of living parts of our personality, of that which may be most valuable in and to us. (Guggenbuhl-Craig 1977, 108)

In other words, the death or sacrifice in marriage is the ongoing process of giving up those aspects of ourselves that we hold most near and dear, and of having to face those aspects of ourselves that feel most crazy and alien. I have suggested that this occurs, not only as a way of achieving an individual "wholeness," but as a way of coming more in alignment with the "third," the unseen body or life form that claims the couple.

The theme of marriage as a form of "death and the maiden" occurs repeatedly in myths and tales. The Greek myth of the rape of Persephone gives a paradigm for the experience of death in marriage. The maiden, Persephone, daughter of the goddess Demeter, while gathering flowers in the fields, reaches for a narcissus and is abducted by Hades, god of the underworld. She subsequently takes a bite of a pomegranate, ensuring that she remain in the underworld as queen. Again, we have the image of an intention toward descent and the experience of depth that "being down" brings. "The death of the maiden" is really the archetypal experience of death held by marriage for bride and groom alike.

In the tale of "Eros and Psyche," an oracle is pronounced that the maiden, Psyche, is to be married to a demonic lover. The preparations for her wedding, are at the same time, for her death.

> The unhappy maid was arrayed for her ghostly bridal, the torches' flame burned low, clogged with dark soot and ash, the strains of the flute of wedlock were changed to the melancholy Lydian

mode, the glad chant of the hymeneal hymn ended in mournful wailing, and the girl on the eve of marriage wiped away her tears even with her bridal veil. (Neumann 1956, 7)

Psyche (soul) accepts her fate and willingly goes to a barren mountain crag to be taken by her demon lover in sacrifice.

Alcestes was the mythological heroine who gave her life in the place of her husband, Admetus. In his poem, "Alcestes," Rilke (1982, 55–59) shifts the event to the wedding day.

> and what came forth was she,
> almost a little smaller than as he knew her,
> slight and sad in her pale wedding dress.
> All the others are just her narrow path,
> down which she comes and comes.

She speaks, not to her husband, but to the god of death, "the original husband."

> no one else has finished
> with life as I have. What is left for me
> of everything I once was? Just my dying.
> Didn't she tell you when she sent you down here
> that the bed waiting inside belongs to death?

Every marriage is a rape of Kore, the virginal bloom, every marriage is Psyche's event, an exposure on the mountain's summit in mortal loneliness, and every marriage is like that of Alcestes, an end of all that we once were, an invitation to the underworld.

Marriage as a form of death is depicted in the myth of Inanna by the descent of Inanna into the underworld. In the myth, the descent occurs out of conventional married life—queen, king, children, and realm. It is as if the more we achieve stability in terms of conventional values, the closer the experience of something radically different arises toward us. The myth reads, "From the Great Above, she opened her ear to the Great Below." Again, as we have seen in Plato and myths and tales, something calls to the soul to go down and the soul descends. Inanna abandons her day-world temples, and prepares herself for the underworld. She puts on all of the investitures of her queenship just as she had put them on for her wedding. As she descends through the seven gates, one by one, she is divested of her crown, beads, breastplate, and so on, the representations of her place in the upperworld, until she arrives in the underworld naked.

Immediately, Ereshkigal, the Sumerian queen of the underworld, fastens the "eye of death" on Inanna.

> Inanna was turned into a corpse,
> A piece of rotting meat,
> And was hung from a hook on the wall.

Inanna, having heard the call from the "Great Below" and having been stripped of her most prized worldly possessions is "hung up," crucified, fixed in the underworld. What does this mean?

Traditionally, the underworld was the home of the dead, the place where the soul or psyche lived after death in the form of a "shade." Depictions of the underworld describe it as "a realm of only psyche" (Hillman 1979d, 46), as opposed to spiritual or material being. Metaphorically, we might say the underworld exists in our lives as that part of our existence that gives us "depth." It is a realm where our usual expectations—which are based on material or spiritual concerns such as the anticipation of well being and prosperity celebrated in marriage—are turned upside down. Marriage as the climax of comedy, from the underworld perspective, might indicate the last joke is on the couple.

The sense of loss integral to the underworld and classically experienced as the abandonment of hope is the sacrifice of rational day-world expectations and preconceptions. Like the divestiture of Inanna's symbols of queenship, the underworld experience requires the sacrifice of upper-worldly ways. For the married couple the sacrifice is the expectation of complete happiness and fulfillment.

The underworld has an integrity of its own. Inanna is told, "The ways of the underworld are perfect. They may not be questioned." In other words, the pain we feel from sacrifice has its own intentions. As a place inhabited only by shades or images, we might say the underworld is metaphorical existence itself, that life that lives us from below, every day, with its larger intentions that go contrary to what we want for ourselves. It is what we usually call "the unconscious," a place of darkness and dimness where orientation is difficult, a place of no desire or progression, where heroic modes of acting, handling, and conquering don't work. Instead, as a realm of shades or shadows, it is a place of being, reflecting, imagining, fantasizing, and remembering.[2]

The story of Orpheus and Eurydice helps us in our understanding of the underworld of marriage. When Orpheus wed Eurydice, the god of marriage, Hymen, attended, but it was said that he was gloomy and did not sing his songs. Later Eurydice was bitten by a snake and died, descending

into the underworld. Orpheus's grief was so great that he went to the underworld to retrieve her. There he so charmed the king and queen of the underworld, Hades and Persephone, with his playing of the lyre, that they consented
to his taking Eurydice with him, provided he did not look back at her.
Inevitably, Orpheus looked back and Eurydice returned to the underworld.

Orpheus could be seen to represent our conventional attitude toward
death and the underworld. We want to save ourselves and others from its
influence, but the underworld seems to have its own power and its intentions take us over and present themselves to be "under-stood." Eurydice
might be seen to embody the underworldly attitude. In his poem, "Orpheus.
Eurydice. Hermes," Rilke (1982, 49–53) describes her as not being concerned with upperworld life, rather, he depicts her as "pregnant" or "full"
with the perfection of death.

> She was deep within herself, like a woman heavy
> with child . . .
> Deep within herself. Being dead
> filled her beyond fulfillment. Like a fruit
> suffused with its own mystery and sweetness,
> she was filled with her vast death. . . .
> She had come into a new virginity
> and was untouchable; her sex had closed
> like a young flower at nightfall. . . .
> She was no longer that woman with blue eyes
> who once had echoed through the poet's songs,
> no longer the wide couch's scent and island,
> and that man's property no longer.
> She was already loosened like long hair. . . .
> She was already root.
> And when, abruptly,
> the god put out his hand to stop her, saying,
> with sorrow in his voice: He has turned around—
> she could not understand, and softly answered
> Who?

The Eurydice of the underworld is complete in herself. She doesn't
require anything beyond what is at hand. She doesn't need the expediency
of heroic action or the charm of artistry. Immediacy is itself a world for her.
Day-world concerns pass her by and when they focus on her, she departs
again without remorse.

In Ereshkigal, Inanna meets the Eye of Death, the power of immediate apprehension that instinctually "sees through," that is immediate, complete in itself, nonconceptual, noninterpretive. In the face of the eye of death, Inanna is crucified, corpsed, left for rotting and putrification. This is the time of being "hung up," "stuck," when there is no movement in the marriage, just the feeling of slowly being "cooked" or "tamed," the meanings held by the original Greek sense of "to marry."

Inanna is freed when Enki takes dirt from under his fingernail and fashions creatures who are able to enter the underworld as flies and obtain Inanna's release by repeating the moans and groans of Ereshkigal suffering "with the cries of a woman about to give birth." What frees up the situation is the focus on small things "at hand"—little feelings and sensations and the ability to empathize.

Marriage to the Underworld

A replacement is needed for Inanna in the underworld. She goes back to the upperworld and comes upon her servant, Ninshubar, and her sons, Shara and Lulal, all of whom have been affected by her stay in the underworld as they dress in the sackcloth of humility. The one figure who hasn't been affected is the king, Dumuzi, who remains in his shining kingly garments. His inability to be influenced by or hear the World Below attracts that very world, the Eye of Death, to himself. Inanna "fastened on Dumuzi the eye of death" and the gala—the underworld henchmen, who "know no food" or drink or gifts or lovemaking or family, who do not know good from evil and show no favor. The gala just get things done no matter to whom they are in service or what the cost, and they attack Dumuzi in ritual dismemberment. This is another crucifixion of Christ, the slaying of the god/king/lover for the sake of wholeness in the individual, completeness in the marriage, fertility in the community—the sacrifice of heroic ways that have become stagnant, rigid with pride, and rutted in habit.

Dumuzi escapes and dreams many omens of impending disaster. He hides in the grass, among the plants, and in the ditches. Like Nebuchadnezzar, he is brought from his pride, which closes him off to the world, down to earth. He is caught but escapes again and hides in an old woman's house and, finally, in his original home, the sheepfold, where he is caught, stripped, and nailed. With Dumuzi driven back to his original condition, the crucifixion, the slaughter of "the wild bull" is made complete.

Inanna mourns the loss of her husband, but she is instructed by a fly, born in dung and small enough to go anywhere, where she can find him.

She discovers Dumuzi alone on the edge of a barren steppe, takes him by the hand, and tells him that for half the year he is consigned to the underworld. The myth ends with praises, not to Inanna, but to Ereshkigal, queen of the underworld.

In the end, married life may be "happily ever after" for some, but more commonly it is an expression of the underworld, a place where the underworld emerges—leaving two people just together, hand in hand at the edge of a desert, on a fundamental barren plane of existence, looking, not at each other, but at a world with which they have now become a part. Through the death of relationship, individual, heroic being has been opened to a more encompassing form of being with the world.[3]

We have now seen death secretly and aesthetically at work in our lives through forms of technolgy and ritual and through generational and romantic relationship. Finally, we turn to death in its more overt and visible manifestation—the appearance of violence and the phenomenon of race.

PART FOUR

Death as Visible

CHAPTER SEVEN

The Necessity of Violence

> God is a man-eater. For this reason men are sacrificed to him.
> —Gnostic Gospel of Philip (62–63)

> Jesus said, "Men think, perhaps, that it is peace which I have come to cast upon the world. They do not know that it is dissension which I have come to cast upon the earth: fire, sword, and war."
> —Gnostic Gospel of Thomas (16)

The subject of violence evokes violent reactions, indicating it is a psychological event that requires a perspective different from our usual, ego-based predilections and attitudes. An orientation of psyche (soul) would stay close to the experience at hand, especially experience that is repugnant, uncomfortable, or traumatic. From the standpoint of soul, we need to address violence on its own ground, rather than banishing it or repressing it with an attitude of "zero tolerance."

Soul encompasses paradox, and violence carries many paradoxes that violate our need for a comfortably self-certain perspective. We want to control violence, but violence comes in its own time and speaks its own language. We associate violence with evil, yet it has always been a central aspect of our religious, political, and domestic life. Violence both terrifies and fascinates us. We want to rid ourselves of violence, yet we commonly resort to violent measures as solutions, worship violent icons, communicate through violent acts, and are entertained by violent images.

We want to distance ourselves from violence, locating it in war and terrorism halfway around the world, but then a building is bombed in our own heartland. We want the bombing to have been perpetrated by Middle Eastern terrorists, but we find the boys next door as the primary suspects. We want violence located away from us in streets of another part of town, perpetrated by members of a different race from a different socioeconomic class. In Boston, when a young white woman is murdered and her white husband describes the perpetrator as a young black male, there is a public outcry—until the killer is revealed to be the husband himself. The fact is that the most dangerous place to be is in one's own home, and the most dangerous people are members of one's own family.

We want to fix violence to categories such as poverty and biology, mental illness, gender, and age. When a suburban Texas housewife and mother is brutally butchered in her own home with over forty blows from an ax, the image of a madman comes to mind, yet the murderer turns out to be not a male psychopath, but another suburban housewife and mother, a neighbor and close friend of the victim. The fact is that the hormone that is associated with human aggression is not the male sex hormone, testosterone, but a neurotransmitter, serotonin. In the United States violent acts against spouses are actually committed as much or more by women than by men. In addition, the many shootings, rapes, and throwing of infants out of windows by young people have drawn our attention to the violence of children.[1] In sum, violent behavior cannot be exclusively linked to race (Shacter and Seinfeld 1994; Van Soest and Bryant 1995), poverty (Fraser 1996), mental illness (Siegfried 1996), gender (McNeely and Robinson-Simpson 1987), or biochemistry (Gladwell 1997).

In the United States we tend to think of violence as a contemporary problem, but violence has been a moral issue throughout our history. Richard Maxwell Brown describes the urban ethnic violence in America of the 1830s, 1840s, and 1850s as "a period of sustained urban rioting . . . (which) may have been the era of the greatest urban violence that America has ever experienced" (Hofstadter 1970, 14). In 1838 Abraham Lincoln felt moved to speak of "the increasing disregard for law which pervades the country—the growing disposition to substitute the wild and furious passions in lieu of the sober judgment of courts, and the worse than savage mobs, for the executive ministers of justice" (Williams 1980, 5–6).

We want to find causes for violence, but violence eludes our need to situate and control it. We want to associate violence with television and movies, but while most of the Western industrialized nations watch the same television programs and movies, the United States has a homicide rate much greater than that of any other. We want to trace violence to our frontier origins, yet the more peaceful nations of Canada and Australia had beginnings in equally rugged environments. We want to think of violence in terms of crime, forgetting that contemporary violence more often takes the form of automobile accidents, road rage, and air rage experienced by all of us. We want to connect violence to environmental conditions, yet anthropology tells us that cultures living in the same geographical area can be either warlike or peaceful (Meade 1949). We are drawn to images of man-made explosions and crashes in newspapers, movies, and television, but for ages, violence was rendered by gods and goddesses in the form of natural forces—earthquakes, lightning, floods, hurricanes, tornadoes. The natives of Indonesia worship the volcano as god, and as Wolfgang Giegerich (1985) has reflected, for years our primary god-image was the atom bomb.

We think of violence as destructive, while in fact we use it for many creative purposes. It is at the heart of many creation myths, including that of contemporary science with its theory of the "big bang." What we think of as "urban development" consists of the violent demolition of older buildings that hold our history. The construction of structures such as highways and dams involves the destruction of ecological habitats and places sacred to indigenous populations. Our modern relationship to the earth and its resources has been that of perpetrator.

In contemporary life, where we are engulfed in media noise, talk is show, and "communication" is a form of god, no one listens, and violence serves as a means for "being heard." In 1992, George Lott entered a court building in Fort Worth and commenced firing a pistol, killing two and wounding others. He then went directly to the local television station to turn himself in as if he needed a channel for expressing his side of a court case he had lost. Louis Lapham (1995) observed that the same week that a federal building was bombed in Oklahoma as a message to the government, Robert McNamara's book came out describing the bombing of North Vietnam as a means of sending a message to that country. The bombing of Vietnam was coming at about the same time that inner-city youths were concocting Molotov cocktails, giving their own expression of rage. The same week that the Federal Building was bombed, bomb as message was literalized in a mail bombing by the unabomber in Sacramento. The contemporary confusion of communication, self-expression, self-fulfillment, and violence is expressed in the statement of the mad bomber played by Dennis Hopper in the film *Speed:* "The being of the bomb is unfulfilled if it is left unexploded."

We live in a society founded upon competition and individualism. When our values are individual success and well being at the expense of others, then there are always losers, without a place to contain the experience of loss except through violent retaliation. Individuality inevitably involves violent invasion of others' individuality, raising the question as to whether "freedom" and "equality" can co-exist.[2]

We are exploring the paradox of the great extent to which violence encompasses our lives in relation to our denial of violence as a part of ourselves. Violence is an underlying core of our identity as a culture and tolerated as a solution as much as it is abhorred. A more detailed inquiry shows violence to be an integral part of our identity in four major areas: (1) the role of violence in our Judeo-Christian heritage, (2) the inherited values concerning violence in the historical emergence of the United States as a country, (3) the traditional violent nature of domestic life in Western civilization, and (4) the cross-gender nature of violence.

Violence Has Us

1. Violence and the Judeo-Christian Tradition. We want to believe that our major theological influence, the Judeo-Christian tradition, gives us a foundation for living in peace and harmony. The fact is that much of the Bible is steeped in the violent actions of an angry God, in blood and in warfare. The Old Testament begins in murder when God honors the offerings of the hunter-brother, Abel, and not the offerings of the farmer-brother, Cain. In jealousy, Cain kills Abel. God wants blood, and God gets blood. Regina Schwartz (1997) points out that the identity of the Hebrew people as the children of Yahweh was founded in violent imagery in the covenant between God and the Hebrews. The Hebrew phrase for "he made a covenant" is *karat berit,* meaning "he cut a covenant." Each of the rituals of the covenant involves violence—Abraham's cutting of animals in two and passing fire between the parts, the cutting of human flesh at circumcision, the scenes at Mount Sinai where words are cut into stone, and Moses' casting the "blood of the covenant" toward the people (Exodus 24: 3–8).

God tends to His new Creation by wiping out civilizations with floods and cities with fire. He commands a loyal servant to kill his only son in bloody sacrifice. He sends plague, disease, and predators onto the Egyptians before finally killing their firstborn children and wiping out their army. He punishes his own children by having three thousand of the unfaithful slaughtered for worshiping the golden calf (Exodus 32: 25–29), by burning the sons of Aaron to death when they use the holy fire wrongly (Leviticus 10:2), and by causing the earth to swallow whole families and burning 250 who have been unfaithful (Numbers 16:31–35). He justifies himself simply by saying, "I kill and I make alive" (Deuteronomy 32:39).

The Hebrew people establish their homeland through a series of holy wars filled with violent takeover—Joshua's sacking of the cities of Jericho (Joshua 6:21) and Ai (Joshua 8:26–29)—and violent actions such as that of Jael, a woman who drives a stake through the head of a sleeping enemy chief (Judges 4:21). One of the Psalms in praise of God is a song of revenge against the Babylonians: "Happy shall be he who takes your little ones and dashes them against the stones" (Psalm 137:9).

The New Testament centers on a man we think of as the "Prince of Peace," yet he is also a violent revolutionary. Jesus is born in a sea of blood,[3] and he says explicitly that he does not come in peace but with a sword (Matthew 10:34). Jesus throws moneychangers out of the temple (Mark 11:15) and prophesies its destruction (Matthew 24:2). When Jesus says "all they that take the sword shall perish with the sword," we want to read this as a plea for nonviolence, forgetting that Jesus has previously called himself the sword and knew that he would die. Jesus' death through torture, dismemberment, and bloodletting is one of the most gruesomely violent images in all of religious history and a central icon of Western culture. The Biblical story ends with a series of apocalyptic acts of total destruction.

We are seeing that in the Judeo-Christian tradition, one of the ways in which Divinity makes its presence known is by violent "break in." In the history of Christianity this violence is made human. As Schwartz has suggested, a monotheistic religious attitude is more prone to violence because it engenders a singular viewpoint as analogue to one overarching god. This single ground then must not only be defended against everything which it is not, but promoted through conquest. We think of Christianity as the civilizing force of the Western world, yet the establishment of this civilization came about against a bloody backdrop of barbarous actions, persecutions, and righteous warfare.

2. *Violence in America.* Americans don't remember well. When we talk about violence as a social problem to be overcome, we forget that we are a culture of violence in history, attitudes, and belief systems, and in our use of violence as a means to wealth and power. It is not that America is unique in this tradition, but what is noteworthy is the depth and pervasiveness of violence in American life in conjunction with America's sense of innocence and virtue. The following section, which touches upon various aspects of violence in America, is meant as a reminder.

Although the interface between whites and Native Americans has been extremely complex from the early encounters of the Pilgrims with local natives into the twentieth century, the predominant spoken and unspoken

attitude of whites toward Native Americans has been one of violent confis-
cation and genocide (Brown 1971). In 1803 Thomas Jefferson wrote of his
intention to force Native Americans into an agricultural way of life that
would lead them into debt so that a "cession of lands" to the whites could
come about (Time-Life 1997, 60). In 1830 Andrew Jackson, desiring the
"disappearance" of Native Americans, signed the Indian Removal Act,
institutionalizing involuntary relocation that eventually included forced
marches wherein stragglers were shot, masses were chained and loaded
into boxcars, and concentration camps were the final destination. In the
latter half of the nineteenth century General Philip Sheridan's statement,
"the only good Indian is a dead Indian," was acted out in scores of mas-
sacres and attempts at overt extermination of entire tribes. At the turn of the
century, Theodore Roosevelt wrote, "The most ultimately righteous of all
wars is a war with savages, though it is apt to be also the most terrible and
inhuman. The rude, fierce settler who drives the savage from the land lays
all civilized mankind under a debt to him" (Jacobson 1998, 218). The
Eisenhower Commission on violence summarized that broken treaties,
unkept promises, slaughter of defenseless women and children, and the
taking of scalps characterized the white American mode of encountering
Native Americans.

American culture finds a second founding cornerstone in the violence
done to another ethnic group, African Americans. Although the subject of
slavery in America is quite complex (Berlin 1998; Blackburn 1997; Thomas
1997), the fact remains that slavery was institutionalized violence conducted
against blacks in America for centuries. In the 1700s slave revolts in northern
states were punished with torture and burnings. During the draft riots in New
York City in 1863, just months after the Emancipation Proclamation, there
was wholesale murder and lynching of blacks. Throughout Reconstruction
there were violent clashes between black and white militia groups in the
South. After Reconstruction, the practice of lynching blacks became commonplace, often a regular weekend event in some southern communities, until
well after the turn of the century. Racial conflict found expression in urban
race riots—Chicago in 1919, Harlem in the 1930s, Detroit in 1943, Harlem,
Detroit, and Los Angeles in the 1960s, and Los Angeles and Miami in the
1990s. Racial violence was renewed during the civil rights movement of the
1960s with the murders of Medgar Evers, Martin Luther King Jr., Bobby
Hutton, and civil rights workers in the South, as well as systematic acts of
violence taken against individual members of the Black Panther party by
police, FBI, and other agencies of the government.

America's move from agriculture to industry was achieved at the expense of a long history of violence, starting with the great railroad strike in 1877 and extending through the years into the industries of mining, lumbering, railroad car manufacturing, textiles, and steel. Taft and Ross have identified over 160 instances where state and federal troops have intervened in labor disputes, and they conclude that "the United States has had the bloodiest and most violent labor history of any industrial nation in the world" (Hofstadter 1970, 19).

America as a political entity was founded in violent rebellion and Americans are traditionally violent over governing principles and policies including: conflict between Pilgrims and Puritans in the seventeenth century, colonial riots against unfair British taxes in the eighteenth century, the Civil War, riots against the draft in New York in 1863 and again a hundred years later in the Vietnam era, the violent acts of the Weathermen and anti-war groups in the 1960s and the violence of government against these and more peaceful groups, and the recent violent acts taken by civilian militia, religious fringe organizations, and groups espousing racial hatred.

The tradition of the vigilante committee is a form of violence particular to America wherein extralegal action is undertaken in support of community values. Historically, groups of citizens have taken enforcement of the law into their own hands ostensibly for the purpose of protection, but often for the sake of self-justified violence (Brown, R. 1969).

Americans have a tradition of settling individual, family, and religious conflicts with violence—the duel of Alexander Hamilton and Aaron Burr, gunfights between factions on the frontier, the feuds between families such as the Hatfields and McCoys, and the persecution of groups such as Quakers and Mormons.

America has a long history of violence by enraged and disenfranchised individuals in the form of assassinations and mass murders. Of the last twenty-six presidents, four have been murdered in office and four more have been the target of gunfire during their time in office. The rash of mass murders by individuals in the United States in the late 1900s might be seen as expression of our own "terrorist" tendencies. Random and mass killings were inflicted on the campuses of the University of Texas and the University of Oregon, at a McDonald's in San Diego and a cafeteria in Waco, on a New York commuter train, in schools in Arkansas and Colorado, and in public places in Salt Lake City and Atlanta.

Violence by individuals mirrors the official violence conducted by American government agencies: the use of atomic warfare against a civilian population, President Johnson's bombing of North Vietnam in a war he knew could not be won, the resort to warfare in the Persian Gulf where two hundred thousand Iraquis were killed, the use of violent means by agencies of the government against the Branch Davidians in Waco and individuals at Ruby Ridge, and the systematic beatings by police of ethnic minority individuals like Rodney King.

America is a "gun culture" and a central feature of violence in the United States is the tradition of the right of private individuals to bear firearms. The Revolutionary War was won by a militia of citizens using their own weapons. The Second Amendment to the Constitution guarantees the right of private citizens to bear arms, but this amendment was written to serve a civic, not an individual, need for a citizens' militia. There was one gun for every 10 colonists; now there is more than one gun for every individual American. Guns serve as a response to individual anxieties and as a symbol for equalizing power and control of destiny in a society where power and control are available to only a few. Every day in the United States, 4,000 new handguns are produced, and more than 220 million firearms are in circulation. Statistics on death by firearms range from over 13,000 people killed by handguns annually (over 100 times the rate of Canada, the next nearest country ("Status of Guns" 1995)) to 87 people killed daily by gunfire (Slater, 2000). During the past 20 years, nearly half a million Americans have been murdered and 2.5 million have been wounded by gunfire of any type (Schlosser 1997). Currently, 70 percent of the murders in America are committed with a firearm (Schlosser 1997). Children in the United States are 12 times as likely to die by gunfire as any other industrialized country (Ryan 1997).

D. H. Lawrence wrote that "the essential American soul is hard, isolated, stoic and a killer" (Hofstadter 1970, 27). H. Rap Brown said that America is as violent as it is apple pie. James Schlessinger Jr. has called Americans "the most frightening people on this planet" (Schlessinger 1968, 19). A metaphor from the film *Speed* seems to fit the American culture. A mad bomber has rigged a bomb onto a bus so that it will go off if the bus goes under fifty miles per hour. If we slow down, we will explode.

3. Domestic Violence. One of the most paradoxical aspects of violence is the fact that it occurs more often than not between people who know each other and especially family members. The policy of informing neighbors of known sexual abusers of children, for example, is contraindicated by the fact that most sexual abuse of children is conducted in the home of the children (Fiorenza and Copeland 1994, 4). Of those convicted of sexual assault of children, only 10 percent are strangers—33 percent are parents, 40 percent are acquaintances, and 13 percent are family members other than parents

(Sharp 1996). Half of the injuries stemming from willful acts of violence are inflicted by someone known to the victim ("Domestic Violence Figures Rise" 1997). Seventy-five percent of mass murders are conducted by killers who know their victims (Diamond 1996, 4). Forty-one out of forty-four homicidal victims and offenders are not strangers (Palmer 1974, 91). Nine out of ten women murdered in the United states are killed by men known to them, 72 percent in their own homes (Fiorenza and Copeland 1994, viii).

Domestic violence in the West has its historical antecedent in ancient Greek culture. Hannah Arendt informs us that the ancient Greeks distinguished between freedom in the political order and necessity in the household. Force and violence were considered justified in the sphere of the household because they were the only means available to master the necessities of home life, liberating one for the relative freedom of political life (Arendt 1969, 31).

4. Violence and Gender. In Western culture historically, domestic violence has been institutionalized as gender-related. The first marriage laws of Rome in 753 B.C. stated that women have no recourse but to conform to the temper of their husbands and that husbands control wives as possessions. The traditional concept of the church was that patriarchal power of the husband made him, as the ground of reason, accountable for his wife, the agent of uncontrolled passions. Most European countries historically guaranteed the husband the right to use aggression to control his wife. In the Middle Ages, women were buried alive for threatening husbands or even talking back to them. Later in England, when a husband deemed that his wife could not control her tongue, she was legally liable to be dunked in the public pond. In 1768 Blackstone wrote the English "rule of thumb" whereby a husband could legally beat his wife if he deemed it necessary, but with an object that could be only no wider than the man's thumb.

Recently there have been several studies that throw a different light on domestic violence, showing that although institutionally domestic violence is gender-related, in fact men and women both have the capacity for violence. In 1977 Rodger Langley and Richard Levy, authors of a previous classic on wife beating, found that one out of five American married women have beaten their husbands and cited FBI statistics stating that there is a 50–50 gender ratio related to spouse abuse and murder (McNeely and Robinson-Simpson 1987). S. K. Steinmetz (1974) concluded that women were as likely as men to select and initiate physical violence to resolve marital conflicts. (Men because of their greater size and strength are more likely to inflict injury.) Studies by M. Straus and R. Gelles in 1975 and 1985, which were followed up in 1992, indicated that women are numerically more violent and statistically as violent as their male partners (Straus and Gelles 1990). A recent study showed college women are more likely to behave violently toward their male partners than vice versa (Diamond 1996, 52). Finally, we have recently been reminded by the sensational reaction to the cases of Susan Smith and Darlie Routier of a fact that has been commonplace for centuries: that mothers, as well as fathers, kill their children. Mothers commit most child murders (64 percent of their victims are male children) and 82 percent of all people have their first experience of violence at the hands of women (Sewell and Sewell 1997).

Obviously, the fact that mothers have more contact with children is a determining factor, but the point is that violence is not something that can be addressed in terms of gender. Violence appears in all of us, male and female alike. The gender issue is not, "Are men more violent?"; rather, it is the issue of power dichotomy in our culture—"Do we allow women the psychological accessibility to violence in the way we do men, or do we insist that women experience greater guilt and anxiety about their violent feelings?" In addition, do we recognize and acknowledge the inherent violence that occurs naturally in a woman's life, such as the advent of puberty, female sexuality, and childbirth?

I have tried to show how violence "has us" as inheritors of a religious and national tradition that worships and values violence, as carriers of a cultural tradition that locates violence in the home, and as men and women equally prone to violent action. I would now like to review some of the causal explanations of violence that have emerged from different fields of study.

Violence and Reason

1. Biology. Biology explains violence in terms of hormones, sensory systems, and brain structure. People with low serotonin levels are more prone toward impulsive aggression, because serotonin acts neurologically as an inhibitor. (Serotonin cannot be considered as a causal factor because serotonin levels are affected by emotional and environmental factors [Wright 1995].) Aggressive acts in humans can be traced to the limbic system in the brain which, if overstimulated due to damage to the inhibiting influence of the frontal lobe, may be a factor in violent behavior (LoPiccolo 1996; Gladwell 1997).[4] Some psychiatrists and neurologists believe that most vicious criminals are people with some combination of abusive childhood, brain injury, and psychotic symptoms, a view that would bring into question such violent punishment as the death penalty.

2. Psychoanalysis. Various fields of psychoanalysis explain violence in ways having to do with internal psychodynamics. Freud (1972) postulated a set of instincts associated with aggression and ultimately literal death. Otto Rank (1952) hypothesized that the "trauma of birth," the forced separation from the idyllic womb, engenders extreme resentment in the infant. Heinz Kohut (1978) explained rage in terms of an experienced wound to the central core of identity and an associated need for revenge. Eugene Monick (1991), a Jungian analyst, focuses on the threat of castration, the loss of a man's deepest sense of self carried by the symbolic phallus or masculine god-image, as a source of violent anger in men.

Developmentalists look to the early relationship between mother and infant as inherently rageful. D. F. Winnicott (1971) theorizes that the infant has a natural tendency to destroy an object when its needs inevitably are frustrated. It is as if the infant must be able to experience, "while I love you, I destroy you." The ability of the psychological "object," the mothering figure, to survive these acts of intended destruction allows that mothering person to become located outside the omnipotent control of the infant. The infant then no longer has to suffer the need to be in total control of its world. From this view, the "self" is actually formed through a series of destructions.[5]

Psychoanalytic structural theory suggests that, developmentally, the male child needs to attack the father as well as separate from the mother. Karen Horney suggests that males need to keep proving their manhood as a means of development, whereas girls need only identify with the parent of the same sex, the mother, by incorporating the desire to have children. Psychoanalysis generally asserts that the integration of unconscious rage is dependent on the development of adequate ego structure. The ego needs to be strong enough to be able to mediate unconscious affects of rage and emotions of anger so that they may be discharged in an appropriate manner.

3. Anthropology. Cross-cultural anthropological studies in domestic abuse take the stance that domestic violence is not so much a breakdown, but an expression of social ordering, when seen from the perspective of the particular structural values of the culture (Harvey 1994). Violence in some cultures occurs not only between men and women, but between mothers and daughters, between sisters-in-law, and between various family groupings as an accepted form of relatedness. Violence in the service of gender idioms is frequently used to order differences in identity through power hierarchies between the two genders. Men may use violence aggressively, while women use it defensively. Violence may be acceptably used by men in some cultures as a result of perceived threat to their identity as men.

Domestic violence can be utilized as part of a larger cultural tradition of ritual violence between groups or in interaction with the supernatural. In the Alto Xingu of lowland South America, gang rape is a religious practice, and in some tribes in the Andes violence is part of community regeneration (Moore 1994). In these cases, violence reflects an attitude that some aspects of humanity are similar to supernatural powers that cannot be controlled.

4. Existential Psychology. From the perspective of existentialism, violence as a basis of being serves as a form of self-definition for those who have been disempowered. Rollo May (1972) asserts that violence is bred in powerlessness and is an escape from the void of impotence. Violence unites the self in action, organizes the self, brings about an identity, a personal will to autonomy, and self-determination. Violence extends from a need to "touch," to connect with the other, when there is need for contact and little sense of its possibility. Jean-Paul Sartre refers to violence as "self-creating" and Frantz Fanon considered violence as a "creative madness" when used by disenfranchised peoples. "Violence alone, violence committed by the people, violence organized and educated by its leaders, makes it possible for the masses to understand social truths and gives the key to them" (Fanon 1963, 33). From the existentialist perspective, violence—throwing down the lance in aggressive self-assertion—separates and creates "self" as it creates "other."[6]

Although causal explanations can give a sense of control and self-certainty in attempting to come to terms with the subject of violence, their very multiplicity in conjunction with the many ways that violence appears give rise to the sense that there is something about violence which *encompasses* us. Perhaps the irrational core of violence indicates it can't be explained through notions of causality conceived through reason. With a larger sense of violence in mind, we would ask how we can talk about violence as a display of something that transcends reason and cultural structures. What might be the transcendent purpose or necessity in violence? How does violence violate and abuse our habitual way of seeing? Is it possible that violence can deepen our way of being?

Violence and Archetype

> Terrifying are the attent sleek thrushes on the lawn,
> More coiled steel than living—a poised
> Dark deadly eye . . .
>   —Ted Hughes, "Thrushes"

Etymologically the word "violence" has many connotations aside from our usual associations of force and destruction. It stems from the Latin *vis*, meaning force and strength, as well as vigor, vitality, and the comic spirit of *vis comica*. It is also connected to *vim*, meaning energy. The Latin *violare* means infringe upon, disregard, and abuse, whether physical harm is done or not. The Latin *violentia* connotes vehemence and impetuosity, as well as the more familiar sense of violation, a physical force inflicting injury upon or damage to persons or property. It is also the improper treatment of a word, a perversion of meaning, an unauthorized alteration, or undue constraint.

The Greek antecedents of the word violence are *iov*, which is also the root of the word "violet," the flower used to mark graves, *bia*, which infers bodily strength, force, personified force, and force of the mind, as well as an act against one's will, rape, or preponderating power, *biazo*, to constrain, overpower, dislodge, lay hands on oneself, or contend vehemently, and *biaioz*, meaning death or rape. A cognate of *bia*, *bios*, expands the sense of force to life force in its meanings of life mode, lifetime, livelihood, and life-world. Heraclitus wrote, "The name of the bow (*bios'*) is life (*bíos*), but its work is death" (Wheelwright 1964, 91), indicating the intertwining aspects of life and death. The paradox is addressed in a different way in another of Heraclitus' statements, "People do not understand how that which is at variance with itself agrees with itself. There is a harmony in the bending back, as in the case of the bow and the lyre" (Wheelwright 1964, 102). "Bending back" brings music and hitting the mark, life and death, together in harmony. At its etymological roots, violence is associated with the intermingling of life and death.

As we investigate the etymological roots of violence, we begin to move into its larger archetypal or transcendent sense. Jung (1968e) emphasized that experience finds its expression in archetypes, the universal patterns of consciousness and behavior that cross-culturally and throughout the ages show themselves in myth, ritual, religious symbology, literature, and art. Following Jung, we would say that violence appears through archetypal forms. Appearing as it does—suddenly, forcefully, seemingly without cause, overwhelmingly—violence becomes the occasion for the meeting of human with transcendent, the way mortals come to know themselves through encounter with the divine.

Child abuse and infanticide, for example, could well be discussed starting from the background of child sacrifice common in many cultures, and especially in the Hebrew and Near Eastern cultures of antiquity (Wellisch 1954). Martin S. Bergman (1988, 1992), a psychoanalyst, suggests that the sacrifice of the lamb associated with Passover and the rite of circumcision are substitutes for the killing of the firstborn. In other words, what we consider as a social problem, from the standpoint of depth psychology, is derived from a universal pattern.

The facts regarding women as agents of violence in contemporary American culture find their archetypal background in mythical images of violent female figures. The Greek goddess Artemis demanded that bloody sacrifice, *spiragmos,* be made in her honor, and Medea dismembered her own children. Amazons were women of Greek legend who cut off one of their breasts to shoot bows more effectively and who battled men toe to toe. The Gorgons were three sisters with snakes for hair and tusks for teeth whose glance could turn mortals to stone. The Furies were daughters of the Night representative of a primal rage that seeks revenge for injustice done to blood kin. The Harpies were birdlike female creatures with wings and claws who would suddenly sweep in like the wind and snatch away bodies or food, blessing the scene with their excrement. The Maenads were female followers of Dionysus, women from the city who dismembered their families in violent orgy.[7]

In Hindu mythology, Durga is a warrior goddess with ten arms, each carrying a weapon, and Kali is the four-armed goddess of death and skulls, drunk and mad with blood, often depicted in the midst of the severed body parts of her victims. In Egyptian myth Sekhmet is the lioness-headed goddess of war, battle, and vengeance who cries out, "When I slay men, my heart rejoices!" (The human race was saved from her fury only when she confused seven thousand jugs of a mixture of beer and pomegranate juice for blood and became too drunk to continue her slaughter.)

The archetypal "martial maid" (Ruperecht 1974) presents herself in the French heroine Joan of Arc, who after leading the French army to victory and confessing to the sin of heresy, was finally condemned to death for refusing to relinquish masculine clothing. The warrior maiden appears again in the Renaissance poems of Ariosto and Spencer, where women render themselves incognito in armor and then knock men off their horses or fight with them sword to sword. Mary Read and Anne Bonny were pirates who took part in violent exploits on the high seas in the eighteenth century, and in contemporary times, the former East Indian rebel bandit leader, Phoolan Devi, is said to have committed more than a score of murders and over thirty kidnappings.

The archetype of violent womanhood also finds its expression in rituals of other cultures such as the Alto Xingu in South America where, if a man comes too close to female performers during certain rites of passage, he is in danger of attack by groups of women who paint his body, pull his hair, and in some cases gang rape him (McCallum 1994). Among the Yausa tribe of the Trobriand Islands of British New Guinea, the natives declare that if the women in certain wedding ritual groups see a man from another village, they have the right to attack. "The man is fair game of the women for all that sexual violence, obscene cruelty, filthy pollution and rough handling can do to him" (Malinowski 1929, 274). Forced intercourse, defecation and urination in the face of the man, abuse and laceration of his body are all part of the practice.

Nowhere can we get a clearer sense of how violence is archetypally a part of family life than from the foundational works of Western literature, the Greek tragedies. The most complex of these stories is that of the House of Atreus, depicting family violence passing from one generation to the next.

A man is granted the extraordinary favor of dining with the gods. He responds by inviting the gods to a feast in which he feeds them the dismembered body of his own son. The gods are outraged and restore the son to life. He, in turn, has two sons who eventually kill a step-brother to please their mother and are banished. Subsequently one brother seduces the other's wife, but the deceived brother prevails in a conflict over rule of the city, and the seducer is banished. He is subsequently retrieved by his brother who takes further revenge by feeding the seducer the body parts of his, the seducer's, own children disguised in a stew. The seducing brother is again banished and in his wanderings, unknowingly impregnates his own daughter. In ignorance, she marries her uncle, the murderer of her siblings and bears the child of her father.

Years later the father is apprehended, brought to prison, and his unknowing son is sent to kill him. The two discover they are father and son. When the mother of the son finds out that the imprisoned man is not only father of her child, but her own father, she kills herself. Her son revenges his father, who is also his grandfather, by killing her husband, the king, his uncle. The two sons of the now dead king drive their uncle and cousin away and kill another son of their uncle. One brother marries his cousin's former wife, smashing the head of her infant child in the process and the other brother marries her sister.

When the sister is abducted by enemies, her brother-in-law, the king, sacrifices his daughter to appease the gods so that his army can sail in quest of retribution. The mother of the sacrificed daughter, in collusion with her lover, the cousin of her husband and the murderer of her father-in-law, takes revenge by killing her husband upon his return from the war. The avenging mother and her lover, in turn, are killed by the now-avenging son and daughter of the mother. The avenging son is pursued by the Furies until finally being acquitted of the crime in exchange for the enshrinement of the Furies.

The dynamics in this image of family life, which we now attempt to understand through the designation "dysfunctional family" and control through the prescription of family therapy, indicates there is something of archetypal necessity in the household that wants blood. Blood carries the dual meaning of life and death, reflecting harmony and discord in human relations. Clytemnestra, the mother who murders and is murdered, has a dream wherein she gives birth to a snake, lays it in swaddling clothes, and takes it to breast. She is horrified to find "the creature drew in blood along with milk." We hunger for blood as well as for milk; we thirst for vengeance as well as nurturance; and we look first to domestic life to have these needs satisfied.

Greek tragedy tells us that behind our institutions of home and court lies a need for sacrifice as connection with the divine. The root of the word "sacrifice," which means "to make holy," is the Hittite word *saklais,* which means "rite." The gods give blood and want blood in return. Archetypally speaking, one way the human soul creates itself is through blood sacrifice. "The soul first made itself through killing," says Wolfgang Giegerich, in a statement based on the fact that hunting has been a part of the human condition during 95 percent of human history. Giegerich quotes Walter Burkett, "not in pious conduct . . . is the God experienced most powerfully, but also in the death blow of the axe, in the blood trickling off . . . the fundamental experience of the sacred is the sacrificial killing" (Giegerich 1993, 7). Hubert and Mauss concluded from a study of sacrificial rites that "in sacrifice is the genesis of gods" (Girard 1977, 89). In Hebrew one of the words for sacrifice, *korban,* is associated with the word *karov,* to bring together. In other words the underlying intention of sacrifice is to bring humans together as they come into connection with the gods.

Rene Girard (1977) makes the connection between violence and the sacred explicit. For Girard, sacrifice contains a religious mystery and a practical function. "Violence is not to be denied" (Girard 1977, 4), and when there is sacrifice, the entire community is protected from its own violent impulses. "Violence will come to an end only after it has had the last word and that word has been accepted as divine" (Girard 1977, 135).

Jung demonstrated in his early writings that sacrifice as an archetypal situation is a renunciation of ego strivings that are inherent in everyday feelings of depression. The sacrifice of the regressive striving for a former passive, protected condition results in the creation of self and culture. Jung said, "The world comes into being when man discovers it. But he only discovers it when he sacrifices his containment in the primal mother, the original state of unconsciousness" (Jung 1956, 417). Jung gives an example of violence as sacrifice of the ego in "The Visions of Zosimov," an alchemical text that depicts the psychological torture of a priest giving himself over to spiritual being (Jung 1967). In this account one finds images of the skin flayed from the head, bones burned in a fire, eyes popping out, pools of blood forming in the sockets, and flesh spewed forth—all displayed as a mode of attaining spiritual well being. Jung sees this sacrifice as a mode of transformation from an attitude centered in the ego to one attuned with a more highly developed level of being.

Sacrifice is one of the core features of initiation. Young people universally separate themselves from family and community in order to reenter as adults, renewed in a knowledge of the mysteries. Most cultures provide rituals for young people to achieve this passage through a process of encounter and often identification with monsters, enemies, death—and subsequent return. Young men may become "beserkers," putting themselves in a transcendent state of voracious ecstacy by donning skins and dancing in wild, rageful, homicidal fury that is contained within ritual.

When there are no meaningful rituals through which young people may enter adulthood, archetypal forms find their own way. Violence and suicide among youth is a way for young people to step outside cultural norms and face violent dangers and death itself. Mass homicide in Cambodia and Africa carried out by adolescents may be seen in this light. Street gangs have existed for as long as there have been cities. Renaissance Italian cities were constructed with passageways crossing above the streets so that citizens could avoid the gangs below. The following is a description of street gangs in 1741 in Hamburg, Germany: "In the town the street boys ruled . . . in an almost intolerable manner. . . . No horse remained untormented, no stagecoach was safe. . . . They would throw (newly imported firecrackers and rockets from East India) into the stagecoaches full of fancy ladies and gentlemen. Whigs, toupees . . . and velvet coats would burn or be completely ruined from the fireworks. Then the godless horde of boys would shout with joy, split up, run and disappear" (Guggenbuhl 1996, 9–10).

Contemporary gangs of boys and girls find their identity by associating themselves with a certain neighborhood to be defended as if it were a mother country. With the ready availability of handguns, youth violence becomes initiation gone deadly. For black males within the group aged 15–24, homicide is the leading cause of death (Shacter and Seinfeld 1994, 347). The combined homicide and suicide rate in the United States for all men ages 15–24 is 3 times that of the general population ("Homicides Decline, But Toll Is Heaviest on Young Men" 1995). The murder rate for young men of this age has tripled since 1960 and is 35 times as high as that of Great Britain (Schlosser 1997).

The archetypal perspective allows us insight into another aspect of violence: ethnic violence as love for the blood of the mother, mother country, or kinship. James Hersh (1985) suggests that the culminating image in the story of the House of Atreus, the trial of Orestes for the slaughter of his mother, Clytemnestra, in revenge for the death of his father, is a dramatizing of the conflict between *ethnos* and *polis*. *Ethnos* represents the memory and love of a people for the bloodline of the mother and the intimate connection with the particularity of geographical places as represented in rituals where sacrificial blood is poured into the earth. Violence in Ireland, the Balkan countries, Africa, and the Middle East could be said to be ruled by this principle. Clytemnestra represents the innate ties of kinship, and the Furies who have been plaguing Orestes give voice to the bloodline's thirst for revenge. *Polis*, in contrast, is the place of language and written contracts where there are conceptual structures of consequences for actions and where one makes one's name, not through action, but in words. The vengeance of *ethnos,* at its etymological root, is a kind of rageful wind trapped in the stomach, while *polis* is a more sublimated place of dialogue. The two sides come to a compromise formulated by Athena when it is agreed that Orestes will be freed, but the Furies will be remembered and honored in sanctity.

We have seen that violence creates self, but it also takes one outside self. Throughout Western tradition, which values rationality and self-control, to be "beside oneself" is associated with possession by evil spirits and the devil. The devil, however, has a dual character. Our word "devil" comes from the Greek *diabolos, diabollein,* meaning "to tear apart." Rudolph Otto points out that "ferocity is the origin of Lucifer . . . fury . . . the mysterium tremendum" (Otto 1950, 106), but the word "Lucifer" means "light bringer." The word "satan" means "one who obstructs," from the Hebrew *malak,* the shadow of the Lord, but Satan was always an angel, originally thought of as sent by the Lord to perform tasks on earth, even those that human beings might not appreciate. Satan originally carried "spirit energies," forces that organize all natural process (Pagels 1995, 40, 143).

We think of possession as demonic. The idea of the demonic originally comes from the Greek sense of the *daimon.* Christian influence through the ages has led us to associate demonic with evil, but the Latin translation is *genii,* to generate or to beget. Heraclitus said that man's character is his *daimon.* In Plato's sense the *daimon* is a mediary from the gods to earth. The word means to divide or distribute and originally referred to momentarily perceptible activity of the divine, like when a horse is startled for no apparent reason. Jung states that the *daimon* is a determining power that comes upon man from outside, like providence or fate (Jung 1959, 27). When one is possessed by the demonic, a kind of self-organizing, asserting, generating power is gathered that can be both frightening and fascinating. *Endaimonium* is the ability to live with the demonic, to integrate opposing forces of love and hate and assimilate them through an honoring of the demonic in our daily existence, admitting it into our thinking and imagination.

We are talking about violence in terms of its place in archetypal forms of gender, domestic relatedness, sacrifice, initiation, the call for memory of mother blood and earth, and the redemptive aspect of its association with the devil. With archetype as background we can now come back to violence in everyday experience. Gaston Bachelard has written on the work of Isidore Ducasse as an epistemology of violence reflecting the essential animal nature of humans. Bachelard imagines the "animal life complex" in humans as the aggressive energy that seizes the moment and creates it. In this sense humans hold the possibility of existence through the "explosive joy of the moment of decision" (Bachelard 1986, 10). Violence is manifest any time there is an approach to a situation through "the will to attack displayed in all of its essential frank hostility" (Bachelard 1986, 3). Here human being is animal being. "The will to lacerate, claw, nip and squeeze in the fingers" is what is fundamentally human (Bachelard 1986, 19).

> We never know where a gesture will discover its corresponding paw, fang, horn or claw. . . . It is the dynamics of exact aggression that determines the most appropriate beast (and) . . . at that point . . . all of animality is at his disposal. (Bachelard 1986, 11)

At the same time, the give and take of animal being in the world allows for thinking and comprehension. "There is nothing in the understanding that was not first in the muscles" (Bachelard 1986, 60). Animal being brings about change because "the imagination cannot comprehend a form except by transforming it, by dynamizing its becoming, by seizing on it like a section of the flux of formal causality" (Bachelard 1986, 89).

Robert Sardello helps us understand the relationship between violence and imagination by reminding us of the ancient Greek concept of *thymos,* the raging of blood in the lungs, manifesting in the world through enactment. *Thymos* is derived from the verb *thuein,* to make smoke, to offer sacrifice, as well as to act violently, to run wild. *Thymos* is the generator of motion, that which arouses one to action in the world, the home for joy, love, and anger. Related to the word *thymos* is our word "enthusiasm," from the Greek *entheos,* a form of possession accompanying ritual ecstacies. If we can see our every encounter with the world as an enactment of *thymos,* then, like the world, we are constantly undergoing transformation through violent disruption. Sardello writes:

> The heart of the dramatic imagination of the world is this violent reforming of the cosmos and when it is possible to really feel the soul of the world, meeting it with soul, a restructuring of soul results. There is no better description for this restructuring than violence. . . . When set in motion in the world, imagination diffuses and disperses in unknown, unsuspected forms. Imagination as meeting the world explodes in a thousand pieces. (Sardello 1992, 143)

Bachelard and Sardello are echoing Martin Heidegger's insight regarding the fundamental relationship between violence and being. As we encounter our being, as we discover, uncover, invent, create, formulate, we are at once "breaking out" of an old world and, ourselves, "breaking up" and "gathering" together at the same time.[8] These actions are not facilities of ours, rather we are acting as modifying conduits of primordial forces, enabling the revealing of essences. Like primordial man, as agents of violence, we are "opening up ourselves" to being as the disclosure of a world. Heidegger: "The violent one, the creative man, who sets forth into the un-said, who breaks into the un-thought, compels the unhappened to happen and makes the unseen appear—this violent one stands at all times in venture" (Heidegger 1959, 135).

Here we are seeing that humans cannot be beings in the world authentically, that is, through imagination, unless that imagination is housed in a violent mode. Just as Jung says that any coming to consciousness is a violent event, Bachelard, Sardello, and Heidegger are saying that meeting the world, change, creation—all are violent happenings.

Violence and Memory

Hannah Arendt has said that "only sheer violence is mute and for this reason violence alone can never be great" (Arendt 1969, 26). For Arendt, true freedom is the ability to live with ambiguity. We have been working to see that violence has us and how it finds its place with us. How can we best hold ambiguity, best develop relationship with violence? In *The Iliad,* Homer depicts violence in vivid images as a way of life of the courageous warrior, but also shows that it can be carried to excess and can only be stopped through a reflective decision, animated with the emotion of grief shared between two men, to allow a burial to take place. In *Antigone* tragic strife between generations can only be ended through burial.

Burial is the primordial act of memory. Among the last words of Oedipus before he leaves the earth in resolved departure are "Remember me," words echoed by the restlessly wandering ghost of Hamlet's dead father. The representatives of spilled mother blood, the Furies, ask that the slain mother be remembered and they are only appeased when they are given a place to be remembered themselves. Burial and enshrinement evoke reflection, memory, and imagination—all aspects of action in the Greek sense of finding the right word at the right moment—and literal action is brought to a momentary close.

Why is violence part of the soul's "necessity"? The Indo-European root of the word *ne-ked-ti* means "no drawing back." There is no retreat from violence. When three women roll back the stone and find Jesus unburied, an omen is revealed of the two millennia of violent unrest to follow in the name of the hero battling fear. We don't want fear, but violence teaches us to fear. Jung tells us that with fear comes creation and new consciousness. Heraclitus said that war *(polemos)* is the father and king of all things, the aboriginal creator. And what is it that is feared, and what is it that is created? The Greeks saw it in the struggle, "Know thyself." Jung describes "self" as the "original man" or the "son of man." "This Man (is) loving and at peace with all things (yet) warring with all things and at war with itself in all things" (Jung 1959, 218).

CHAPTER EIGHT

The Soul of Race/The Heart of Color

In beginning this final chapter, I would like to summarize some of the themes that have run through the book. We start with the split in the modernist, rationalist mind that attributes "consciousness" or soul to the interiority of individual being and assumes the world or culture to consist of lifeless external factors that impinge upon and affect the individual. As a result, when we think of change, we are split. "Care of the soul" (psycho-therapy), imagination, reflection are reserved for the interiority of individual being, while change in the world is brought about through heroic means—advocacy, enlightened humanism, directive education, social action, strat-egy planning, growth through development. Since we don't imagine the world as having a life of its own, it is deprived of our imagination and reflection, and is left to withstand our frontal assaults.

An alternative to these ontological assumptions can be found in other cultures and in forgotten remnants of the Western tradition—the idea of *anima mundi* "the life of the world." This alternative, which finds its origi-nal Western home in Platonic philosophy (just as psychotherapy does), would locate soul or autonomous life in the world itself (Hillman 1982a; Moore 1992; Sardello 1992). In this sense, the external world or culture would not be a derivative, a sublimation, or an acquired collection of things, beliefs, and values. Rather, it would be seen as having a life of its own, each thing, event, and situation having an existence with intentions that are separate from ours. What we refer to as "social problems" would be symptomatic indicators of this autonomous life—"depressed" economy, "anorexic" urban landscape, "congested" roadways, "hazardous" waste, "polluted" air, "rampant" crime, cultural "attention deficit disorder," collec-tive "addiction" to medication, "hysterical" public emotional life, "manic" lifestyle, and "split" value systems. From this standpoint, we would see the world reflected in the pathology of the individual, as well as be able to practice therapy on the world.

In the tradition of psychotherapy, depth psychology has brought a unique dimension to our sense of the reality of the psyche, the notion of an unconscious life. For Freud and Jung the psyche involves more than conscious awareness, namely, an unseen dynamic in the depth or invisibility of our being. This dynamic involves the working of influences more powerful or painful than our ordinary consciousness is able to allow, which I am characterizing as a feeling of death. From the standpoint of depth psychology a sensitivity to the soul of the world would invite a reflective therapeutic focus on the unconscious life of the world in its multiple layers of history and values. Such an endeavor reveals the world to express itself through universal patterns or forms that I have attempted to describe in relation to television, ball games, relationship, fathers and sons, and violence. Presently we look at race as another example of the appearance of death through the workings of a structure larger than our ability to control or to understand through reason.

The Psychology of Race

Michael Adams (1996), in his book, *The Multicultural Imagination: "Race," Color and the Unconscious,* asserts that depth psychology and its many schools of psychoanalysis have mostly ignored the factor of race in unconscious life. Whereas Freud called our attention to the importance of sex and childhood experience and Jung to the spiritual and teleological aspect of the psyche, Adams argues that the significance of race, racism, and raciality in our unconscious has been neglected, and he builds a strong foundation for a psychological exploration of these factors. For Adams, "the clinical *is* the cultural," and he enables us to see that culture can be approached clinically.

Adams frames the central theoretical question of racism as, "Is race real?" There are differences among peoples in appearance, cultural heritage, attitudes, and values, and, in the case of minorities, the ability to survive in an oppressive culture. Adams takes the position that race does not objectively exist and that any reference to race is a displacement of underlying cultural assumptions. This position rests heavily on the notion that psychological meaning is often a matter of projection. We take a physical aspect, such as color of skin or texture of hair, and arbitrarily attribute to it positive or negative value based on our unconscious assumptions. For example, while "going black" has historically taken on a negative connotation in white British and

American culture, there was a period of time in the late 1960s when anything black was fashionably preferred by liberal whites. By the same token, hair texture of black people has taken on significantly different symbolic meanings for blacks, whether naturally "kinky" or groomed straight, depending on particular underlying values.

Matthew Frye Jacobson (1998) gives an historical/political account of race in America showing how race has been a prevailing idiom for discerning citizenship. In this sense race has been a central organizing structure in the service of power. In 1790 Congress passed a law stating that "all free white persons who, have, or shall migrate into the United States . . . shall be entitled to the rights of citizenship" (Jacobson 1998, 22). During the period of greatest migration, 1840–1924, race as a mode of perception as well as a tool of power was focused upon various European peoples to their detriment—Slavs, Jews, Poles, Greeks, Italians, and most particularly the Irish. The result was a deep tension between established perceptions of all Europeans as "white" and the need to revise the definition of whiteness based on a variety of social and political circumstances of the moment. This tension culminated in the passing of the immigration act of 1924 in which quotas were established favoring the peoples of northern and western European nations.

Racism, as a set of assumptions projected onto physical appearance and assumed to be inferior, has deep historical and philosophical roots not only in America, but in the Western world as a whole which have been traced by Lucius T. Outlaw (1996) in his book, *On Race and Philosophy*. Outlaw follows the thought of Arthur O. Lovejoy, which regards racism as a derivative of the long-lived philosophical idea of "the great chain of being." Plato (*Timaeus*) held that a transcendent unity of being manifested itself in the multitude of living things. Aristotle formulated the stance that each thing not only had its own "nature," but that there was a continuity among the multitudes of qualities that could be arranged in a hierarchical order according to degree of perfection. "Some are marked for subjection, others for rule" (*Politics* I, 5, 1254A 18–24). In the Enlightenment the idea of a hierarchical chain of being lent itself to justifications of inequality as evidence of the discriminating nature of "Infinite Wisdom." Kant wrote:

> The Negroes of Africa have by nature no feeling that rises above the trifling. Mr. Hume challenges anyone to cite a single example in which a Negro has shown talents, and...although many of them have been set free, . . . not a single one was ever found who presented any . . . praiseworthy quality. (Outlaw 1996, 192)

Decades later Hegel referred to Africa as "the land of childhood . . . enveloped in the dark mantle of Night" (Outlaw 1996, 57–58). At the same time, the Romantic idea of equality among the many, when subjected to the influence of Darwinism, easily turned into political notions of social superiority. In the nineteenth century, "race" became a category of hierarchical ordering.

In America, the Founding Fathers were presented with the dilemma of asserting the right of all people to freedom while maintaining the institution of slavery. Paradoxically, the ability to promote freedom, thought of in terms of liberty from British rule, was most pronounced among those who were economically independent of England due to the practice of slavery. The distinct physical "nature" of blacks gave rise to a notion held by Jefferson, Madison, Monroe, Jackson, Clay, Webster, and Lincoln, among others, that, given "the degrading privation of equal rights," it would be impossible to admit blacks into the body politic. Alexis de Tocqueville, the great commentator on American society in the early 1830s wrote: "the two races are fastened to each other without intermingling; and they are alike unable to separate entirely or combine" (B. Schwartz 1997, 69).

Outlaw points out how underlying the modernist conception of intellectual superiority of whites is the assumption that reason is the supreme value. In other words, "reason," considered to be the ability to separate oneself analytically from environment and from oneself, that is, to be self-conscious, is the *logos,* or "center of being" for the European mind. Hegel wrote:

> (The) distinction between himself as an individual and the universality of his essential being, the African in the uniform, undeveloped oneness of his existence has not yet attained. . . . The Negro . . . exhibits the natural man in his completely wild and untamed state. (Outlaw 1996, 58)

Detached, self-conscious reason as the highest value of humanity has dominated the Western tradition from Plato (in part) and Aristotle through Augustine and Aquinas into the Enlightenment and the evolution of science, resulting finally in the Industrial Revolution, which gave whites an economic and technical advantage over other races and translated into racist superiority. This attitude can be detected in the early thinking of the young "human" sciences of anthropology and psychology in the early twentieth century. Anthropologist Lucien Levy-Bruhl (1910/1985) focused his work on the distinction between "primitive" and "civilized" peoples. Levy-Bruhl considered the former to be "pre-logical" in the sense that he perceived "primitive" people to confuse subject and object in a form of "participation mystique."

In addition, the "primitive" mind was dominated by collective values. "Primitive" people did not gain identity through individualistic reference as did white, rational, Western man, but through identity with collective structures, images, and values.

Jung, more than any of the other founders of the psychology of the unconscious, struggled with the psychology of race. Jung considered the unconscious to have two major aspects: (1) the strictly personal historical residue of experience and (2) the source of universal patterns of consciousness and behavior or the collective unconscious. In other words, for Jung, we are unconsciously motivated by the forgotten memories and desires of our personal life, but more important by those memory traces and dynamics common to all of humanity. We are distinctly personal individuals, but at the same time and more profoundly, we are connected to all of humanity by common archetypal structures. I am guided by the same images, consciousness, and action patterns when I cross the busy, urban street, as the aboriginal native crossing the turbulent river.

Most of Jung's focus on unconscious life is through his notion of the collective unconscious, which he saw as a form of universal memory that crossed all boundaries of culture and extended throughout the ages. He thought the spiritual crisis or neurosis of modern life was due to our alienation from aspects of the collective unconscious that he thought of as "primitive" or "primordial." In other words, whereas Freud returned us to the childhood of our personal life, Jung returned us to the origins of our collective life. He used the metaphor of the "original man" or "archaic man" to describe this deepest level of psychological life, with which we needed to be in relationship in order to realize the "totality" of our being.

It is easy to see how Jung, as a white European, steeped in the rational tradition of philosophy and science, would see native peoples, particularly black-skinned people of Africa and African descent as metaphors or signifiers for the primal being of the collective unconscious. He felt compelled, in fact, to take several trips to visit native peoples in different parts of the world, as a way of experiencing the collective unconscious outside the European mind. One of these trips was to Central Africa, where, happening to see a black native standing alone on a rock in the early morning sunlight, he had the following experience:

> I was enchanted by this sight—it was a picture of something utterly alien and outside my experience, but on the other hand a most intense *sentiment ju deja vu.* I had the feeling that I had

already experienced this moment and had always known this world which was separated from me only by distance in time. It was as if I were this moment returning to the land of my youth, and as if I knew that dark-skinned man who had been waiting for me for five thousand years. (Jung 1961a, 254)

Jung saw the inherent value of what he considered as alien to whites in the lifestyle of modern black people in America. From his trips to America in the first decades of this century, he noted that white Americans were unconsciously fascinated and influenced by black people. He observed this in the way Americans walked, talked, and laughed and in American music and the communal, public quality of American life.

Just as the coloured man lives in your cities and even within your houses, so also he lives under your skin, subconsciously. Naturally it works both ways. . . . Every Negro has a white complex and every American a Negro complex. . . . The white man hates to admit that he has been touched by the black. (Jung 1964, 508)

Jung believed that the reason that whites and blacks in America were psychologically intertwined was that each carried the "inferior" or unconscious aspect of the other. What was undeveloped in each was seen as inhabiting the other. Therefore, one race cannot live in conjunction with the other without considerable ambivalence.

For Jung, both the "primitive" black African man and modern black people represent aspects of the unconscious of modern whites for which they have a simultaneous attraction and repulsion (and vice versa). What is unconscious has a fascination for us because of the psychic energy it holds, but we also resist it because whatever is "other" than we know about ourselves is frightening. This ambivalence can be seen in Jung himself during an event on his visit to Africa. While attending a native dance Jung joined in the dancing, but as the night wore on, became anxious for his safety and perceived the dancers as becoming a "wild horde."

I called the people together, distributed cigarettes and then made the gesture of sleeping. Then I swung my rhinoceros whip threateningly, but at the same time laughing, and for lack of any better language I swore at them loudly in Swiss German that this was enough and they must go home to bed and sleep now. (Jung 1961a, 271–72)

Here we can see Jung courting his unconscious (as seen in the natives) but resistant and fearful at the same time.

Jung was struggling to transcend modernist, European rationalism with a Romantic vision of the unconscious as a realm of originary being with all of its primal energy (and terror) as represented in part for whites by the "primordial man" as well as by black people in general. He also maintained a grounding in the realm of logocentric rationality, which gave rise to several unfortunate aspects in his psychology of race. He followed Levi-Bruhl in seeing native peoples as having a less psychologically developed consciousness in their "participation mystique" with their environment. He accepted as valid his own assumptions that certain characteristics were inherent to black people—physicality, rhythm, and emotionality. He regarded "going black" as a psychological danger, in that it involved identifying with deeper layers of unconsciousness. In sum, Jung's wrestling with race reveals the conflict between his Romantic and rationalist tendencies.

Jung's struggle with race does give us an important psychological insight. We gather our own sense of self through encounter with an "other." Other people serve as supplements in the formation of our own identity. White or black, we fear knowing ourselves, and the anxiety expresses itself through fear of others. To the degree that we can be empathic with the alien "other," to that extent we can know ourselves. Conflict between races reflects conflict between different aspects of ourselves.

"Raciality" as Difference

Although his dominant focus was the universal aspect of the unconscious, Jung did delineate multiple aspects of the unconscious in emphasizing its complexity beyond the personal. Among these aspects are realms of collective experience particular to each race, nation, tribe, and family (Jung 1953, 147–48). The idea that there is something psychologically real about race, something inherent in us that loves common ancestry and for which we would die, all symbolized in the image of "blood," has been echoed repeatedly in the ongoing contemporary discourse involving race (Outlaw 1996).

As mentioned in the previous chapter, James Hersh (1985) raises the question of the place of the identity of a people, race, or nation in the modern world. Hersh looks for a response to this question in the origin of the city-state or *polis* in ancient Greece, an event that brought together divergent tribes under one governing body. Hersh considers the Oresteia trilogy by Euripides (*Agamemnon, The Libation Bearers, The Euminides*) and its

culmination with the trial of Orestes for the murder of his mother, Clytemnestra, as giving voice to different sides of the conflict. The Furies who
pursue Orestes state the case of the principle of *ethnos* or "mother blood."
Ethnos (meaning "nation" or "race") represents the memory and love of the
bloodline of the mother. In contrast, the principle of the *polis* subverts all
ethnic differentiations in the service of abstract, contractual law. In the trial
of Orestes, the voice of the *polis* is given by the god of reason, Apollo. The
city became the place where use of language in dialogue and contract took
priority over justice through revenge, and the principle of reason as the
highest value emerged. In framing the problem of race in terms of a debate
between *ethnos* and *polis,* Hersh is telling us that we are today engaged in
an archetypal conflict between two universal viewpoints, each with its own
validity.

In this light, we would look to Outlaw's phenomenological approach
to race. He states from the outset that

> it is important to consider raciality (as opposed to racism) and
> ethnicity as real, constitutive aspects of determinate populations
> of human beings . . . (and) as important resources for continuing
> efforts to critically (re-)construct and maintain social realities.
> (Outlaw 1996, 1–2)

For Outlaw the historical and sociological realities of blacks provide a
separate and distinct "life-world" to be explored, described and validated.
He cites the great black thinker and writer W. E. B. Du Bois, who wrote "The
Conservation of Races" in which he outlined a program to find the meaning
of race for black people. In speaking of race, Du Bois emphasized that

> no mere physical distinctions would really define or explain the
> deeper differences—the cohesiveness and continuity of these
> groups. The deeper differences are spiritual, psychical, differences,
> undoubtedly based on the physical, but infinitely transcending
> them. (Outlaw 1996, 6)

Du Bois focused on the need to understand the "forces" that "bind together"
people of a "common blood," that is, people (1) of biological descent from
common ancestors, (2) holding common history, laws, ideals, and religious
values, and (3) with common patterns of thought and action.

Following Du Bois, Outlaw suggests that different ethnic groups give
different meaning to life events, creating separate and distinct "life-worlds"
or cultures. For Africans and people of African descent to recover their own

life-world would mean reviving a logic distinct from pure reason in which, as Leopold Senghor states,

> knowledge . . . is not the superficial creation of discursive reason, cast over reality, but discovery through emotion: less discovery than re-discovery. Knowledge coincides, here, with the *being* of the object in its discontinuous and indeterminate reality. (Outlaw 1996, 67)

In the language of depth psychology, we would say that the recovery of a life-world, or a psychology of "raciality" (Adams 1996; Outlaw 1996), is a retrieving from unconsciousness or a revealing of the archetypal reality of ethnic distinctions—those histories, values, and habitual ways of thinking and doing that are held in common throughout the ages by people of the same race.

The Heart of Color

> Coal black is better than another hue
> In that it scorns to bear another hue
> —Shakespeare, *The Tragedy of Titus Andronicus*

If we are validating raciality as difference we inevitably are confronted by physical appearance, most obviously by the color of skin, and by the question, "Is color real?" Historian Winthrop Jordan (1977) states that the first use of the term "white" to characterize an ethnic group occurred in the early 1600s after English sailors had their first contact with black Africans. The first impression of the English regarding Africans had to do with the blackness of their skin, making the English cognizant of the whiteness of their own skin. The skin color of the Africans made an emotional impact on the "white" English because blackness carried the association of dirty, ugly, evil, deadly, and devilish, while white carried the associations of clean, beautiful, good, lively, godly. Immediately the opposition of white and black and the association of white as superior and black as inferior came into play.

The idea that there is a universal tendency among cultures regardless of skin color to see the colors white and black as opposed suggested by the critic of culture Tzvetan Todorov (1993) is supported by studies such as those of linguist Charles Osgood (1957) and anthropologists Brent Berlin and Paul Kay (1969). Etymological and linguistic analyses suggest that the color white carries a universal signification of superiority (Hillman 1986).

The Indo-European root of white means "to be bright." The Greek phrase "a good day" means a white day, and Plato associated white with the gods (*Laws* 12:956a). Dominique Zahan (1977), an expert on African peoples, states that in black African countries white is traditionally associated with lightness, heaven, harmony, joy, home, abundance, and food. Human beings are thought to be white before entering the world and a good, affable, pleasant person "has a white belly." Anthropologist Victor Turner (1967) reports that among the Ndembu of Central Africa, white is the dominant color, and he lists twenty-five superior qualities associated with white, including goodness, making strong and healthy, purity, without misfortune, power, to be without death, to be without tears, authority, meeting with ancestor spirits, life, health, and begetting young.

Adams points us to a telling passage related to the color white in Herman Mellville's *Moby Dick*. The narrator, Ishmael, is speaking of the "whiteness of the whale" and notes the many ways in which white is associated with divinity by many cultures. He also notes how whiteness "strikes more of panic to the soul than the redness which affrights in blood." In fact, white "heightens . . . terror" and is a "crowning attribute of the terrible." It is the "common, hereditary experience of all mankind . . . to bear witness to the supernaturalism of this hue" (Melville 1980, 190–92). Ishmael senses that white is the most "appalling" to mankind as a "colorless all-color" because it is representative of the "great principle of light," the indicator of the frightening infinity of the universe.

The color black, in Black Africa, symbolizes work, pain, uncertainty, and doubt (Zahan 1977). Among the Ndembu, Turner lists evil, bad luck, suffering, disease, witchcraft, death, sexual desire, and night as being associated with black. In the Western world, black traditionally carried the meanings of dirt, soil, foul, malignant, death, disaster, sinister, atrocious, horrible, wicked, disgrace, and liability to punishment (Hillman 1986).

Racism, then, can be seen as a problem having to do with unconscious conflicts not only in ethnic but also in color qualities. Both Zahan and Turner refer to color, for example, not in the scientistic sense of secondary refractions of light, but as "whole realms of psychobiological experience" (Turner 1967, 91). From this standpoint, color refers to a substantive condition, way of life, or "world." In Africa, whiteness is associated with the purity of heaven, while blackness is associated with the earth and its travails. Hillman points out that in the cluster of associations around white, there is a hidden morality. White seems to carry the superior aspect of spirit, and does not allow for shadow, shadings, or differentiation. Black writer, Frantz Fanon, declared, "I know only one thing, which is the purity of my conscience and the whiteness of my soul" (Adams 1996, 167). It is no wonder, then, that as Jacobson (1998) suggests, the definition of "whiteness" in the United States is quite fluid and changeable based on the shifting demands of power according to time and place. White provides the ground, then, for exclusive thinking, and from the standpoint of white superiority, something else has to be black and inferior. As Hillman suggests, supremacy is built into the consciousness of the color white, and therefore, white consciousness psychologically *requires* blackness in order to deepen itself.

We are beginning to see that racism, the idea of the superiority of one race over another, emanates from an exclusive identification with the psychological condition of whiteness as purity. The French philosopher, Jean-Paul Sartre, associates white with subjectivist, modern, Western consciousness itself—seeing without being seen, identifying with vision, day, truth, and virtue (Outlaw 1996, 68). To make inroads into racism, then, and to move into what Adams calls "a multicultural imagination" or Outlaw calls an "ethnic philosophy," we would need to be able to imagine not only ethnicity, but color, and especially the color black, in a different way.

Zahan reveals how blackness in Africa is associated with working the earth and the process of maturation. "Like the kitchen utensil whose exterior blackens with use, man attributes increasing importance to the blackness of his skin and this very blackness gives him authority" (Zahan 1977, 74). Hillman (1979d, 1986, 1997a) suggests that the color black in our dreams and daily life represents the emergence of the underworld and psychological "death," not as loss, but as the achievement of a deepened life-world. Blackening indicates that the brightness of the white modernist attitude—disembodied objectivity, self-certainty, reasoned clarity, and naive optimism has been deepened into complexity, distinction, paradox, and mystery. We might call this the "night" world of imagination which white culture confines to art and psychotherapy, but which the world is calling up into the mainstream of its being through the symptom of racial conflict.

In conclusion, Walter Otto gives us our best description of night world as dark light.

The night is a world in itself. . . . A man who is awake in the open field at night or who wanders over silent paths experiences the world differently than by day. Nighness vanishes, and with it distance; everything is equally far and near, close by us and yet mysteriously remote. Space loses its measures. There are whispers and sounds, and we do not know where or what they are. Our feelings too are peculiarly ambiguous. There is a strangeness about what is intimate and dear, and a seductive charm about the frightening. There is no longer a distinction between the lifeless and the living, everything is animate and soulless, vigilant and asleep at once. . . . Who can protect him, guide him aright, give him good counsel? The spirit of Night itself, the genius of its kindliness, its enchantment, its resourcefulness, and its profound wisdom. She is indeed the mother of all mystery. (Otto 1954, 118–19)

And so we end where we began—in the night world. Dark light ultimately is both seen and a way of seeing, image and imagination. Facing the other, vision darkens, deepened by its disturbing presence.

Epilogue

The Four Myths of OJ/The Day of Di

Two events in recent years involving celebrities have galvanized the public imagination to such an extent that we might say an archetype or larger-than-life structure was "in-forming" us through these individuals. In each case, the magnitude of public focus was brought about through a literal death which constellated larger-than-life structures.

"The Four Myths of OJ"

The case of OJ opened like a reprise of scenes from several different classic American movies—the shock of a violent, bloody double murder, the initial investigation, the apprehension of OJ, his escape with the "buddy," public calls for his return, and the final chase/procession with suicide threat, police escort, helicopters, cheering crowds, and home-coming. For months, the subsequent investigation and televised trial gripped the public imagination—but for different reasons, depending on the perspective or myth through which the events were seen. "Myth," here, is a term used to describe a dominant pattern of actions, attitudes, and preconceptions, in short, a larger-than-life structure through which we organize our identity and live out our lives. In this sense the word "myth" means psychological reality. Four major American myths can be gleaned from the variety of reactions to the trial of OJ Simpson for charges of murder of his former wife, Nicole, and her friend, Ron Goldman.

1. Race. Race has always been a factor in the handling of justice in America, and polls throughout the trial leading up to the verdict revealed a distinct and consistent split along racial lines as to OJ's guilt (white) or innocence (black). The racial split in America could not have been displayed in

151

a more dramatic way than by the discrepancy between pictures of groups of blacks in ecstasy and whites in disbelief as the verdict was announced. Norman Mailer (1995) gave a vivid explanation of this discrepancy, citing the difference between the white experience of justice and that of blacks. For blacks, justice is a game in which they are at an inherent disadvantage due to racism and social inequity. For blacks, the "facts" of the case are not so much the mass of details regarding evidence of previous violence, blood and hair samples, and time lines. The more pertinent issue is the reality of fewer financial resources and the history of injustice and discrimination foisted upon them by white-dominated agencies in the judicial system such as the LAPD. For blacks, "real justice" would be the justice of social change.

Chris Darden, the black member of the prosecution team, stated at one of the pre-trial hearings that if use of the word "nigger" was allowed to be an issue in the trial, the outcome would be reduced to a question of whose side are you on, The Man or The Brothers. For blacks, OJ was symbolic as a winner in a white world. The decision regarding his innocence was a power play for blacks, with Johnny Cochran repeatedly playing the race card as trump suit with his blatant appeal for racial solidarity. In sum, one of the contributions of the OJ case was the renewed revelation, especially to whites, of the reality of the black/white power struggle as a dominant myth of our time.

2. *Gender.* Another rallying cry elicited by the trial was that of individuals and groups sensitive to the issue of women as victims in cases of domestic violence. Jeffrey Toobin (1997) has written convincingly of how Marcia Clark, the lead prosecutor, based a large part of her strategy on connecting the evidence of OJ's physical abuse of Nicole with the idea that he would murder her out of his need for power over her. The prosecution dramatically emphasized the 1989 conviction of OJ for spouse abuse and the 911 call that Nicole made in 1993. In past trials, the approach of focusing on the victim had been successful for Clark, but in the OJ case, she didn't adequately take into account evidence that her jury would not want to focus on this topic due to OJ's stature in the black community. A positive outcome of the trial was that it stimulated a call to action for enforcement and laws around issues of domestic violence.

3. *Money.* A third myth-as-reality that finds a home in American society is the discrepancy between justice for the rich and justice for the poor. The trial showed that money is a predominant defining element in contemporary American criminal justice. OJ's lawyers used jury consultants extensively in contrast to the prosecution, and spent large sums on expert witnesses to refute prosecution evidence, all to great effect. Defendants who have money

are able to afford consultants on jury selection who are able to detect the most favorable probable jurors. They can bring in experts to find the inevitable holes in any kind of scientifically based evidence such as laboratory results. Money buys clever lawyers who have perfected the art of trial-as-theater and obfuscate evidence by making investigators look bad and by playing to the emotions of jurors. On the other hand, those without money have less chance of being represented competently and are unable to bring in expert witnesses. They are at a decided disadvantage in the face of the financial resources of the state, and as a result, most criminal cases are decided without a trial through plea bargaining. In the end, the OJ case again raised the issue of whether we should abolish preemptory challenges or even move to a system of professional jurors, as in Europe, which is much less costly and more time-efficient.

4. *Eternal Youth.* Toobin characterized OJ as being a professional at "being OJ." OJ projected a persona to the world that fits a universal image, that of the eternal youth. The eternal youth will always find a way past, through, around, over, and under authority and consequences. Always with a smile, he will cry, "Catch me if you can!", and disappear. The eternal youth has no patience, no time for reflection, and no energy except for his own concerns. The eternal youth carries our spiritual energy, that part of us that wants to soar ever upward to new heights and distances and which can only think in terms of grand schemes that he puts in the center of the universe. This part of us has no time for the "stuff" of life, complexities, problems, hindrances, and the like. The eternal youth will always resist change or development or evolution, while perpetually soaring off, thrust by his own sense of perfection.

As a "shucking and jiving" football player, a television personality running smoothly through crowded airports, and a convicted abusive husband who didn't serve his penalty, OJ avoided consequences. OJ, as "juiced up" phallus, used sex and power as his fuel while he perpetually evaded his fate. Enveloped in his own sense of innocence and charm, OJ perpetually ran from his violent nature and need for control. Nicole said about his reaction to her budding independence, "He'll kill me and 'OJ' his way out of it."

The eternal youth is an image that has a secret place in the heart of a society that is concerned with avoiding long-term planning, social obligations, "infrastructure," taxes, and ecological welfare. It is in the heart of a society founded on its own sense of "manifest destiny" and self-righteous innocence. In a society where the world is excluded and the center is the "self," OJ as self-enchanted star was the twinkle in the public eye.

"The Day of Di"

The astounding outpouring of sadness over Princess Diana's death, a "star-burst" of grief felt by hundreds of millions of people the world over, indi-cates the event to be truly mythical—a happening that activated the deepest layers of the collective unconscious. Diana was a larger-than-life figure who embodied a wide spectrum of human qualities and met our need for an ideal in many areas of life. She was both beautiful and intelligent, strong yet com-passionate, a member of royalty but deeply connected with the poor and ailing.

At the same time that she was an ideal, Diana embodied vulnerabilities that reflected the personal sufferings of each of us as individuals. She had an intense, almost desperate way of searching for love, home, power, and life. She loved her husband, but eventually reacted to his infidelity in kind. She went to extremes to court the right kind of publicity for herself and causes that she favored, and just as intensely she hated the invasion of her privacy by the media. Her last ride, in fact, her last relationship, carried all the earmarks of an impulsive bid for control in which she paradoxically put her life in the hands of a man who had been historically untrustworthy and a driver who was inebriated.

The combination of collective ideal and personal vulnerability allowed Diana to fill several archetypal roles. These are larger-than-life characters, often appearing as images of divinities or legendary people, who display clusters of attitudes and behaviors that are universally similar. In other words, we have a psychological need to align with godlike figures that reflect transcendent areas of human life. Elvis was like the ancient Greek god, Dionysus, who came to town and attracted all the women to his camp, and Marilyn Monroe was like Aphrodite, the goddess of love, inspiring erotic fantasies in men. As Beauty Incarnate, Diana caught the eye of the world. As intelligent and articulate Reigning Princess, Diana had power to change the conditions of the world. As Lady of Compassion, she reached out in public expressions of affection to her children and of sympathy to AIDS patients, mine victims, and the poor, thereby enacting a universal healing ritual of the laying on of hands.

At the same time as Diana presented us with an image of archetypal ideals, she also made public her private sufferings, giving us a larger reflec-tion of our personal wounds. She was betrayed and hurt, not only as a wife and outcast from the royal family, but as a child, hungry for love after the breakup of her family of origin. These painful events fill a universal form—

the Orphan, the Rejected, the Despised—that appears over and over in literature, myths, and folktales. As the Suffering Princess trapped in a tower—rejecting food, pining away in solitary melancholy, giving herself away to dark lovers—Diana was a representation of feeling, physicality, and creative imagination betrayed and trapped in a prison of dead forms and hypocrisy.

Perhaps more than any other larger-than-life figure, Diana most resembled the Greek and Roman divinity who was her namesake. The Roman goddess Diana (or Artemis, her Greek counterpart) was goddess of childbirth and wild animals, who sat at the door of women in the throes of delivery and led her female compatriots in the hunt. The goddess Diana's nurturing qualities were displayed in the multibreasted, ancient sculpture of Diana of Ephesus, just as the nurturing qualities in the princess were displayed in the many photographs of her with the injured, sick, and poor. The goddess Diana lived and was honored outside the confines of civilization, just as Princess Diana ventured outside the well-worn social structures, activities, places, and attitudes of the royal family. The goddess's wild spirit inspired the hunt, just as the spirit of the princess rebelliously fought and defied the staid and rigid expectations of royalty and the invasions of the paparazzi. The goddess, Diana, was jealous of her honors, just as Princess Diana was jealous of her place in the public mind. Above all, Diana was a virgin goddess, and the princess remained untouched by all that she hated. Her last words were, "Stay away from me."

One of the fates of princesses is to be sacrificed. In the Greek myths, Iphigeneia was sacrificed by her father in order to bring wind to his fleet. The Aztecs gave sacrifice to their gods by cutting out the heart of a virgin. Princess Diana married death in several ways. In part, she sacrificed her freedom when she married a prince, she sacrificed her spirit when she entered a royal family, and she sacrificed her individuality in becoming a symbolic figurehead of her country. As the most photographed person in the world, she sacrificed herself by marrying the camera, using it to her advantage and being pursued by it to her death. The phallic camera was the dark lover to whom she was most attached. When she reached too far for it without the containing protection offered by the royal family—like the mythical maiden, Persephone, reaching for the narcissus flower only to be raped by Hades—she was taken into the tunnels of Dis.

As universal princess who seemed to attract even the light of the sun, Diana could not help but also attract the dark forces of the psyche. Egypt has always been the "dark land" to the northern European imagination. Born at the time of the embarrassment of the Suez crisis, Diana perpetuated Britain's Egypt complex by falling for a dark-skinned Egyptian playboy with a history of jilted lovers and creditors. His father had pricked the English skin with his ownership of a traditionally fashionable London department store, his contributions to unpopular politicians, and his purchase of the manor of the former heir to the British throne. Given Prince Charles' open resumption of his relationship with Camilla Parker Bowles, it was inevitable that Diana would react with the unconsciously flaunting choice of a dark lover with money and means to rescue her and take her away from the conflict that would not let her go.

Does our worship of icons indicate a flawed, displaced search for meaning? No, rather it *is* the meaning. We need celebrities to reflect back to us our deepest potentials, needs, and attitudes, as well as our failings, follies, and foibles, and to give us rituals to carry us through the most profound events of psychological life. Diana's funeral was the funeral of the Sacrificed Princess given over to the gods for the transformation and maintenance of the general well being.

Archetypes or divinities *have us,* but at the same time, we make the divine human. The paparazzi are conditioned gadflies, hunters and technicians acting in the service of our need to make celebrities human. The first of the paparazzi was the Greek god Hephaistos, who made a trap for his wife, Aphrodite, in which she was caught in bed with the war god, Ares, and exposed for all the gods to see. To speak of Diana's death in terms of the conflict between freedom of expression and the right to privacy or in terms of the search for meaning in the cult of celebrity, misses something more fundamental. The death of Diana as the Sacrifice of the Princess gives expression to a basic psychological conflict: the gods want to make us divine and we want to make the gods mortal. Diana got caught in between.

NOTES

Chapter 2. Beauty as Appearance

1. Studies show that agreement on what is considered attractive is high and significant both within and outside a single culture (Langlois and Musselman 1995).

2. By contrast the Greeks could be said to have gone to war over beauty when Helen, the most beautiful of mortal women, was taken from them by Paris and the Trojan War ensued.

3. See James Hillman (1979b) for an account of the conference at Nicea in which the Church deemphasized the notion of "soul," which traditionally encompasses both spirit and matter, in favor of an emphasis on a spirit/matter dichotomy that splits inner and outer.

4. Rupert Sheldrake (1988), in his book *The Presence of the Past,* discusses how we can imagine the ground of being in terms of larger forms or "morphic fields" from a scientific standpoint.

Chapter 3. Ball/Play: The Soul of Game

1. Heroes taking their place in eternity is the archetypal theme behind the "hall of fame" for athletes. The German god, Wotan, conducted the first "recruiting" trips when he went around enlisting heroes for his mythical hall of heroes, Valhalla.

2. Our use of warlike terms in football, such as "in the trenches," "the bomb," "the blitz," "captain," "field general," "air attack," and "ground attack" as well as the many allusions to the Super Bowl during the Gulf War by soldiers and politicians, attests to the way that the ball game serves as a substitute for combat.

3. One example of the "larger than" by which we are played is given by contemporary deconstructionists, who would assert that we are played by language. Language is the movement of play which is permitted by the actual lack or absence of a center or origin of consciousness. Play is without security, a surrender to the adventure of the "trace," that which remains available to us through the infinite play of signifiers which is language. (See Derrida 1978).

Chapter 4. Spirit in the Tube: The Life of Television

1. The connection of television to medieval theology can also be seen in the breakup of the contemporary television day with its early morning talk shows, morning soaps, afternoon game-time, news hour, prime time, and late-night talk shows as a parallel to the structure of the monastic day with its *prime, terce, sext, none,* and *vespers.*

Chapter 5. Fathers and Sons: The Perpetually Circling Storm

1. Bach (1973) interprets Esau as sun-hero and his "sacrifice" as representative of the waning of the sun in autumn.

2. Robert Pirsig (1974) portrays this in reverse in his novel, *Zen and the Art of Motorcycle Maintenance,* in the image of a 13-year-old son riding across the country behind his father on a motorcycle.

3. The realization of the importance of bonding between father and children is illustrated in a growing movement to give nonbiological fathers custody rights in cases where it is appropriate (Stevens, A., 1993).

Chapter 6. The Torture of Relationship/The Rites of Marriage

1. All excerpts from the myth of Inanna are taken from Wolkstein and Kramer 1983.

2. See James Hillman's (1979d) chapter, "Psyche," in *The Dream and the Underworld,* for an excellent description of the underworldly mode of being in daily life.

3. In 1986 a poll was taken among married men—80 percent would marry the same woman again. In 1988 a poll was taken among married women—88 percent would marry the same man again.

Chapter 7. The Necessity of Violence

1. The inherent violence of children is explored by William Golding (1954) in his novel, *Lord of the Flies.*

2. Nowhere is this more evident than in the phenomenon of road rage—the result of individuals trapped in metallic bubbles of autonomous individuality, each under the illusion that the wheel of fate is in their hands, while they vie for "right of way."

3. Those who consider contemporary violence in movies as pornographic should visit the cathedral in Sienna, where the slaughter of the innocents is depicted in graphic detail on the floor.

4. This could help explain why, of 25,000 homicides each year, 10 percent are unexplained, unmotivated, irrational acts by total strangers.

5. Michel Foucault (1972) has an analogous view of the unfolding of history in terms of violent ruptures that disrupt fictions of unity and coherence. To paraphrase Foucault, history is effective to the extent that it introduces discontinuity into our being by shattering the familiar landmarks of our thought. This kind of history divides our emotions and dramatizes our instincts; it multiplies our body and sets itself against itself. In short, effective history deprives us of "self" and the reassuring stability of life in the past. It uproots its traditional foundations and disrupts pretended continuity. Knowledge of this sort is not made for "understanding," rather it is made for cutting through.

6. Hannah Arendt (1969) reminds us, however, that what seems like power obtained through violence is not power. Power is the human ability to act in concert; violence is instrumental in character, always in service to something else. The effectiveness of violence in self-defining for Arendt is limited to the meeting of short-term goals.

7. Barbara Ehrenreich (1997, 110) notes that women were among the first hunters.

8. Heidegger (1959, 144) refers to language itself as a "violent gathering."

BIBLIOGRAPHY

Adams, Michael Vannoy. 1996. *The Multicultural Imagination: "Race,"* *Color and the Unconscious*. New York: Routledge.

Agee, James. 1959. *A Death in the Family*. New York: Avon.

Arendt, Hannah. 1969. *On Violence*. New York: Harcourt, Brace and World.

———. 1977. *The Life of the Mind: Thinking*. New York: Harcourt Brace Jovanovich.

———. 1978. *The Life of the Mind: Willing*. New York. Harcourt Brace Jovanovich.

Bach, H. I. 1973, Autumn. "On the Archetypal Complex: His Father's Son." *Quadrant*, 15.

Bachelard, Gaston. 1964. *The Psychoanalysis of Fire*. Trans. A. C. M. Ross. Boston: Beacon Press.

———. 1971. *The Poetics of Reverie: Childhood, Language, and the Cosmos*. Trans. Daniel Russell. Boston: Beacon Press.

———. 1986. *Lautreamont*. Trans. Robert S. Dupree. Dallas: The Dallas Institute Publications.

Beckett, Samuel. 1958. *Endgame*. New York: Grove.

Beebe, John. 1986. "The Father's Anima." In *The Father*. Ed. and with an Introduction by Andrew Samuels. New York: Washington Square Press.

Bennet, Steven. 1985. "A Play of Light or Ben Franklin, The Arsonist." Unpublished paper. University of Dallas.

Benz, Ernst. 1989. *Theology of Electricity*. Trans. W. Taraba. Ed. with an Introduction by D. Stillings. Allison Park, Pa.: Pickwick Publications.

Bergman, Martin S. 1988. "The Transformation of Ritual Infanticide in the Jewish and Christian Religions with Reference to Anti-Semitism." In *Fantasy, Myth and Reality*. Ed. Harold Blum, Arlene Richmond, and Arnold Richards. Madison, Conn.: International Universities Press.

————. 1992. *In the Shadow of Moloch: The Sacrifice of Children and Its Impact on Western Religions*. New York: Columbia University Press.

Berlin, Brent, and Paul Kay. 1969. *Basic Color Terms: Their Universality and Their Evolution*. Berkeley and Los Angeles: University of California Press.

Berlin, Ira. 1998. *Many Thousands Gone: The First Two Centuries of Slavery in North America*. Cambridge, Mass.: Harvard University Press.

Berry, Wendell. 1977. *The Unsettling of America: Culture and Agriculture*. New York: Avon Books.

Blackburn, Robin. 1997. *The Making of New World Slavery*. New York: Verso.

Blake, William. 1965. *The Poetry and Prose of William Blake*. Ed. David Erdman. Commentary by Harold Bloom. Garden City, N.Y.: Doubleday.

Bly, Robert. 1986a. "A Man and A Woman Sit Near Each Other." In *Selected Poems*. New York: Harper and Row.

————. 1986b. "Finding the Father." In *Selected Poems*. New York: Harper and Row.

————. 1987. "The Erosion of Male Confidence." In *Betwixt and Between: Patterns of Masculine and Feminine Initiation*. Ed. Louise Carus Mahdi, Stephen Foster, and Meredith Little. LaSalle, Ill.: Open Court.

————. 1990. *Iron John: A Book About Men*. New York: Addison-Wesley.

Bly, Robert, James Hillman, and Michael Meade, eds. 1992. *The Rag and Bone Shop of the Heart: Poems for Men*. New York: HarperCollins.

Brown, Dee. 1971. *I Buried My Heart at Wounded Knee*. New York: Bantam.

Brown, Richard Maxwell. 1969. "The American Vigilante Tradition." In *Violence in America: Historical and Comparative Perspectives*. Ed. Hugh D. Graham and Ted R. Gurr. New York: New American Library.

Campbell, Joseph. 1949. *The Hero With a Thousand Faces*. Princeton, N.J.: Princeton University Press.

Campbell, Joseph, ed. 1972. *The Complete Grimm's Fairy Tales*. New York: Pantheon.

Carpenter, E. 1970. *They Became What They Beheld*. New York: Ballantine.

Clark, Kenneth. 1956. *The Nude: A Study in Ideal Form.* New York: Pantheon Books.

Colman, Arthur. 1993. *The Father.* New York: Avon.

Cowen, R. 1959. "A Note on the Meaning of Television to a Psychotic Woman." *Bulletin of the Menninger Clinic,* 23, 202–3.

Csikszentmihalyi, Mihalyi. 1990. *Flow.* New York: Harper and Row.

Dante. 1939. *The Divine Comedy: Paradiso.* Trans. J. D. Sinclair. New York: Oxford University Press.

Davidson, Harriet. 1985. *T. S. Eliot and Hermeneutics: Absence and Interpretation in "The Waste Land."* Baton Rouge: Louisiana State University Press.

de Santillana, G. 1969. "The Role of Art in the Scientific Renaissance." In *Critical Problems in the History of Science.* Ed. M. Clagett. Madison, Wis.: University of Wisconsin Press.

de Tocqueville, Alexis. 1956. *Democracy in America.* Ed. Richard Heffner. New York: New American Library.

Derrida, Jacques. 1974. *Of Grammatology.* Trans. Gayatri Spivak. Baltimore: Johns Hopkins University Press.

———. 1978. *Writing and Difference.* Trans. Alan Bass. Chicago: University of Chicago Press.

Diamond, Steven. 1996. *Anger, Madness and the Daimonic: The Psychological Genesis of Violence, Evil, and, Creativity.* Albany: State University of New York Press.

"Domestic Violence Figures Rise." 1997. *The Dallas Morning News,* August 25.

Donne, John. 1954. "The Canonization" and "The Ecstacy." In *Major British Poets.* Ed. G. B. Harrison. New York: Harcourt, Brace and World.

Edgerton, Samuel. 1976. *The Renaissance Rediscovery of Perspective.* New York: Harper and Row.

Edinger, Edward. 1985. *Anatomy of the Psyche: Alchemical Symbolism in Psychotherapy.* LaSalle, Ill.: Open Court.

Edwards, John. 1997. "American Portrait." *The Dallas Morning News,* December 5, A4.

Ehrenreich, Barbara. 1997. *Blood Rites: Origins and History of the Passions of War.* New York: Metropolitan Books.

Ekholm, Susanna M. 1991. "Ceramic Figurines and the Mesoamerican Ballgame." In *The Mesoamerican Ballgame.* Ed. V. L. Scarborough and D. R. Wilcox. Tucson: University of Arizona Press.

Eliade, Mircea. 1958. *Rites and Symbols of Initiation*. Trans. William R. Trask. New York: Harper and Row.

Erickson, Eric. 1963. *Childhood and Society*. New York: Norton.

Esman, Aaron. 1981. "Fathers and Adolescent Sons." In *The Role of the Father in Child Development*. Ed. Michael E. Lamb. New York: John Wiley and Sons.

Esquire. 1989, November. "Bringing Up Daddy," 122.

Fanon, Frantz. 1963. *The Wretched of the Earth*. New York: Grove.

Fiorenza, Elizabeth, and Mary Copeland, eds. 1994. *Violence Against Women*. London: Concilium.

Foucault, Michel. 1972. *The Archaeology of Knowledge*. New York: Pantheon Books.

Fraser, Mark W. 1996. "Aggressive Behavior in Childhood and Early Adolescence: An Ecological-Developmental Perspective on Youth Violence." In *Social Work*, 41(4), 347–61.

Freud, Sigmund. 1950. "Dostoevsky and Parricide" (1928). In *Collected Papers*. Vol. 5. Ed. James Strachey. New York: Basic Books.

———. 1953. *The Future of An Illusion* (1927). Trans. W. D. Robson-Scott. New York: Doubleday.

———. 1957. "Group Psychology and the Analysis of the Ego" (1921). In *A General Selection from the Works of Sigmund Freud*. Ed. John Rickman. New York: Doubleday.

———. 1963. *Jokes and Their Relation to the Unconscious* (1905). Trans. James Strachey. New York: W. W. Norton.

———. 1972. *Beyond the Pleasure Principle* (1920). Trans. James Strachey. New York: Bantam.

Gadamer, George. 1982. *Truth and Method*. New York: Crossroad.

Geertz, Clifford. 1973. *The Interpretation of Cultures*. New York: Basic Books.

Giegerich, Wolfgang. 1985. "The Nuclear Bomb and the Fate of God: On the First Nuclear Fission." In *Spring 1985*. Dallas: Spring Publications.

———. 1988. "The Invention of Explosive Power and the Blueprint of the Bomb." In *Spring 1988*. Dallas: Spring Publications.

———. 1993. "Killings: Psychology's Platonism and the Missing Link to Reality." In *Spring 54: A Journal of Archetype and Culture*. Putnam, Conn.: Spring Publications.

Gillespie, Susan. 1991. "Ballgames and Boundaries." In *The Mesoamerican Ballgame*. Ed. V. L. Scarborough and D. R. Wilcox. Tucson: University of Arizona Press.

Girard, Rene. 1977. *Violence and the Sacred.* Trans. Patrick Gregory. Baltimore: Johns Hopkins University Press.

Gladwell, Malcolm. 1997. "Damaged." *The New Yorker,* February 24, March 3.

Golding, William. 1954. *Lord of the Flies.* New York: Capricorn.

Graham, Hugh, and Ted Gurr, eds. 1969. *Violence in America: Historical and Comparative Perspectives.* New York: New American Library.

Greenberg, M., and N. Morris. 1974. "Engrossment: The Newborn's Impact upon the Father." *American Journal of Orthopsychiatry,* 44, 520–31.

Guggenbuhl, Allan. 1996. *The Incredible Fascination of Violence.* Trans. Julia Hillman. Woodstock, Conn.: Spring Publications.

Guggenbuhl-Craig, Adolph. 1977. *Marriage Dead or Alive.* Zurich: Spring Publications.

———. 1995. *From the Wrong Side.* Trans. Gary V. Hartman. Woodstock, Conn.: Spring Publications.

Halevi, Z'ev ben Shimon. 1979. *Kabbalah: Tradition of Hidden Knowledge.* New York: Thames and Hudson.

Hall, Nor, and Dawson, Warren R. 1989. *Broodmales: A Psychological Essay on Men in Childbirth,* Introducing *The Custom of Couvade.* Dallas: Spring Publications.

Hans, James. 1981. *The Play of the World.* Amherst, Mass.: University of Massachusetts.

Harrison G. B., ed. 1948. "Hamlet." In *The Complete Works of Shakespeare.* New York: Harcourt, Brace and World.

———, ed. 1959. *Major British Writers* Vol. I. New York: Harcourt, Brace and World, Inc.

Harvey, Penelope. 1994. "Domestic Violence in the Peruvian Andes." In *Sex and Violence: Issues in Representation and Experience.* Ed. Penelope Harvey and Peter Gow. New York: Routledge.

Heidegger, Martin. 1959. *An Introduction to Metaphysics.* Trans. Ralph Manheim. Garden City, N.Y.: Doubleday.

———. 1962. *Being and Time.* Trans. J. Macquarrie and E. Robinson. New York: Harper and Row.

———. 1971. "The Origin of the Work of Art." In *Poetry, Language, Thought.* Trans. Alfred Hofstadter. New York: Harper and Row.

Hersh, James. 1985. "From Ethnos to Polis: The Furies and Apollo." In *Spring 1985.* Dallas: Spring Publications.

Hesiod. 1959. *Hesiod.* Trans. Richmond Lattimore. Ann Arbor: University of Michigan Press.

Hillman, James. 1970. "On Senex Consciousness." In *Spring 1970.* New York: Spring Publications.

————. 1975a. "Abandoning the Child" (1971). In *Loose Ends: Primary Papers on Archetypal Psychology.* Zurich: Spring Publications.

————. 1975b. "Betrayal." In *Loose Ends: Primary Papers on Archetypal Psychology.* Zurich: Spring Publications.

————. 1975c. *Re-Visioning Psychology.* New York: Harper and Row.

————. 1975d. "The 'Negative' Senex and a Renaissance Solution." In *Spring 1975.* New York: Spring Publications.

————. 1979a. "An Essay on Pan" (1972). In *Pan and the Nightmare* (with W. H. Roscher). Dallas: Spring Publications.

————. 1979b. "Peaks and Vales: The Soul/Spirit Distinction as Basis for the Differences between Psychotherapy and Spiritual Discipline." In *Puer Papers.* Ed. James Hillman et al. Dallas: Spring Publications.

————. 1979c. "Senex and Puer: An Aspect of the Historical and Psychological Present" (1967). In *Puer Papers.* Ed. James Hillman et al. Dallas: Spring Publications.

————. 1979d. *The Dream and the Underworld* (1973). New York: Harper and Row.

————. 1980. *Egalitarian Typologies versus the Perception of the Unique.* Dallas: Spring Publications.

————. 1981, September. "James Hillman on 'Entertaining Ideas.'" *The Institute Newsletter* 1(1). Dallas: The Dallas Institute of Humanities and Culture.

————. 1982a. "Anima mundi: The Return of the Soul to the World." In *Spring 1982.* Dallas: Spring Publications.

————. 1982b. "Salt: A Chapter in Alchemical Psychology." In *Images of the Untouched.* Ed. Gail Thomas and Joanne Stroud. Dallas: Spring Publications.

————. 1983. "The Fiction of Case History" (1975). In *Healing Fiction.* Barrytown, N.Y.: Station Hill Press.

————. 1986. "Notes on White Supremacy: Essaying an Archetypal Account of Historic Events." In *Spring 1986.* Dallas: Spring Publications.

————. 1987a. "Oedipus Revisited." In *Crossroads.* Eranos Yearbook 56-1987. Ed. Rudolf Ritsema. Frankfurt: Insel Verlag.

————. 1987b. "Wars, Arms, Rams, Mars: On the Love of War." In *Facing Apocalypse.* Ed. Valerie Andrews, Robert Bosnak, and Karen Goodwin. Dallas: Spring Publications.

————. 1997a. "The Seduction of Black." In *Fire in the Stone: The Alchemy of Desire.* Ed. and introduced by Stanton Marlan. Wilmette, Ill.: Chiron Publications.

————. 1997b. *The Soul's Code: In Search of Character and Calling.* New York: Random House.

Hofstadter, Richard. 1970. "Reflections on Violence in the United States." In *American Violence: A Documentary History.* Ed. Richard Hofstadter and Michael Wallace. New York: Alfred A. Knopf.

Homer. 1965. *The Odyssey of Homer.* Trans. Richmond Lattimore. New York: Harper and Row.

"Homicides Decline." 1995. *Dallas Morning News,* October 24.

Huizinga, Johan. 1949. *Homo Ludens.* London: Routledge and Kegan Paul.

Jacobson, Mathew Frye. 1998. *Whiteness of a Different Color: European Immigrants and the Alchemy of Race.* Cambridge, Mass.: Harvard University Press.

Jordon, Winthrop. 1977. *White over Black: American Attitudes toward the Negro, 1550–1812.* New York: Norton.

Jung, Carl Gustav. 1953. "The Relations Between the Ego and the Unconscious" (1916/28). In *Two Essays on Analytical Psychology. CW* 7. Trans. R. F. C. Hull. Princeton, N.J.: Princeton University Press.

————. 1954. "Marriage as a Psychological Relationship" (1925). In *The Development of the Personality. CW* 17. Trans. R. F. C. Hull. Princeton, N.J.: Princeton University Press.

————. 1956. *Symbols of Transformation* (1912/52). CW 5. Trans. R. F. C. Hull. Princeton, N.J.: Princeton University Press.

————. 1959. *Aion: Researches into the Phenomenology of the Self* (1951). CW 9ii. Trans. R. F. C. Hull. Princeton, N.J.: Princeton University Press.

————. 1960. *The Structure and Dynamics of the Psyche.* CW 8. Princeton, N.J.: Princeton University Press.

————. 1961a. *Memories, Dreams, Reflections.* Recorded and Edited by Aniela Jaffé. Trans. Richard and Clara Winston. New York: Vintage Books.

————. 1961b. "The Significance of the Father in the Destiny of the Individual" (1909). In *Freud and Psychoanalysis. CW* 4. Trans. R. F. C. Hull. Princeton, N.J.: Princeton University Press.

————. 1964. "The Complications of American Psychology" (1930). In *Civilization in Transition.* Trans. R. F. C. Hull. Princeton, N.J.: Princeton University Press.

————. 1966. *The Practice of Psychotherapy. CW* 16. Trans. R. F. C. Hull. Princeton, N.J.: Princeton University Press.

————. 1967. "The Visions of Zosimov" (1937). In *Alchemical Studies. CW* 13. Trans. R. F. C. Hull. Princeton, N.J.: Princeton University Press.

————. 1968a. "Individual Dream Symbolism in Relation to Alchemy" (1935). In *Psychology and Alchemy. CW* 12. Trans. R. F. C. Hull. Princeton, N.J.: Princeton University Press.

————. 1968b. "On the psychology of the Trickster Figure" (1954). In *The Archetypes and the Collective Unconscious. CW* 9i. Trans. R. F. C. Hull. Princeton, N.J.: Princeton University Press.

————. 1968c. "Religious Ideas in Alchemy" (1935). In *Psycholgy and Alchemy. CW* 12. Trans. R. F. C. Hull. Princeton, N.J.: Princeton University Press.

————. 1968d. "The Psychology of the Child Archetype" (1940). In *The Archetypes and the Collective Unconscious. CW* 9i. Trans. R. F. C. Hull. Princeton, N.J.: Princeton University Press.

————. 1968e. *The Archetypes and the Collective Unconscious. CW* 9i. Trans. R. F. C. Hull. Princeton, N.J.: Princeton University Press.

————. 1969. "Transformation Symbolism in the Mass" (1940/54). In *Psychology and Religion. CW* 11. Trans. R. F. C. Hull. Princeton, N.J.: Princeton University Press.

————. 1970. *Mysterium Coniunctionis* (1955–56). *CW* 14. Trans. R. F. C. Hull. Princeton, N.J.: Princeton University Press.

Kaplan, Bert, and Dale Johnson. 1969. "The Social Meaning of Navajo Psychopathology and Psychotherapy." In *Magic, Faith and Healing.* Ed. Ari Kirv. New York: The Free Press.

Kennedy, Randall. 1997, May. "My Race Problem—and Ours." *Atlantic Monthly.*

Kohut, Heinz. 1978. "Thoughts on Narcissism and Narcissistic Rage." In *The Search for the Self: Selected Writings of Heinz Kohut: 1950–1978.* New York: International Universities Press.

Kramer, Samuel, ed. 1961. *Mythologies of the Ancient World.* New York: Doubleday.

————. 1969. *The Sacred Marriage Rite: Aspects of Faith, Myth and Ritual in Ancient Sumer.* Bloomington: University of Indiana Press.

Kugler, Paul. 1982. *The Alchemy of Discourse.* Lewisburg, Pa.: Bucknell University Press.

Kuryluk, Ewa. 1997. *Salome and Judas in the Cave of Sex: The Grotesque: Orgins, Iconography, Techniques.* Evanston, Ill.: Northwestern University Press.

Lamb, Michael E. 1981. "The Development of Father-Infant Relationships." In *The Role of the Father in Child Development.* Ed. Michael E. Lamb. New York: John Wiley and Sons.

Langlois, J. H., and L. Musselman. 1995. "The Myths and Mysteries of Beauty." In *1996 Yearbook of Science and the Future.* Ed. D. R. Calhoun. Chicago: Encyclopedia Britannica.

Lapham, Louis. 1995, July. "Seen But Not Heard: The message in the Oklahoma Bombing." *Harper's Magazine.*

Lawrence, D. H. 1961. *The Rainbow.* New York: Penguin.

Lazar, B. 1994. "Under the Influence: An Analysis of Children's Television Regulation." *Social Work,* 39(1).

Lehrs, E. 1985. *Man and Matter.* London: Rudolf Steiner Press.

Levi-Strauss, C. 1973. *From Honey to Ashes.* New York: Harper and Row.

Levy-Bruhl, Lucien. 1985. *How Natives Think.* Trans. L. Clare. Princeton, N.J.: Princeton University Press.

Lingis, Alphonso. 1983. *Excesses: Eros and Culture.* Albany: State University of New York Press.

Loewald, Hans. 1951. "Ego and Reality." *The International Journal of Psychoanalysis,* 32, 10–18.

LoPiccolo, Philip. 1996, October. "Something Snapped." *Technology Review.*

Mahdi, Louise Carus, Stephen Foster, and Meredith Little, eds. 1987. *Betwixt and Between: Patterns of Masculine and Feminine Initiation.* LaSalle, Ill.: Open Court.

Mailer, Norman. 1995. "Black and White Justice." *New York,* October 16, 28–32.

Malinowski, Bronislaw. 1929. *The Sexual Life of Savages in North-Western Malasia.* New York: Harcourt, Brace and World.

Mander, J. 1978. *Four Arguments for the Elimination of Television.* New York: Quill.

May, Rollo. 1969. *Love and Will.* New York: Norton.

———. 1972. *Power and Innocence: A Search for the Source of Violence.* New York: Norton.

McCallum, Cecilia. 1994. "Ritual and the Origin of Sexuality in Alto Xingu." In *Sex and Violence: Issues in Representation and Experience.* Ed. P. Harvey and P. Gow. New York: Routledge.

McCarthy, K. 1990, November. "TV Addicts Not Lured to Shows, but Medium." *The American Psychological Association Monitor.*

McGuire, W., ed. 1984. *Dream Analysis: Notes of the Seminar Given in 1928–1930 by C. G. Jung.* Princeton, N.J.: Princeton University Press.

McLuhan, Marshall. 1964. *Understanding Media: The Extensions of Man.* New York: New American Library.

McNeely, R. L., and G. Robinson-Simpson. 1987. "The Truth About Domestic Violence: A Falsely Framed Issue." *Social Work,* 32(6), 485–90.

Meade, Margaret. 1949. *Male and Female.* New York: Dell.

Megill, A. 1985. *Prophets of Extremity.* Berkeley: University of California Press.

Melville, Herman. 1980. *Moby Dick.* New York: New American Library.

Merleau-Ponty, Maurice. 1962. *Phenomenology of Perception.* Atlantic Highlands, N.J.: Humanities Press.

Miller, Arthur. 1949. *Death of a Salesman.* New York: Viking.

Miller, David. 1970. *Gods and Games: Toward a Theology of Play.* New York: Harper and Row.

———. 1981. *Christs: Meditations on Archetypal Images in Christian Theology.* New York: The Seabury Press.

Milton, John. 1957. *John Milton: Complete Poems and Major Prose.* Ed. Merritt Hughes. Indianapolis: Bobbs-Merill Educational Publishing.

Minnow, Newton. 1962. Speech to National Association of Broadcasters, May 9, 1961. *Equal Time,* 52.

Mitschedlich, Alexander. 1973. *Society Without the Father.* Trans. Eric Mosbacher. New York: Jason Aronson.

Monick, Eugene. 1991. *Castration and Male Rage.* Toronto: Inner City Books.

Moore, Henrietta. 1994. "The Problem of Explaining Violence in the Social Sciences." In *Sex and Violence: Issues in Representation and Experience.* Ed. Penelope Harvey and Peter Gow. New York: Routledge.

Moore, Thomas. 1992. *Care of the Soul: A Guide for Cultivating Depth and Sacredness in Everyday Life.* New York: HarperCollins.

Neumann, Erich. 1956. *Amor and Psyche: The Psychic Development of the Feminine.* Princeton, N.J.: Princeton University Press.

Nouwen, Henri. 1972. *The Wounded Healer: Ministry in Contemporary Society.* Garden City, N.Y.: Doubleday.

Ong, Walter. 1967. *The Presence of the Word.* New Haven: Yale University Press.

———. 1982. *Orality and Literacy.* New York: Methuen.

Onians, R. 1951. *The Origins of European Thought.* Cambridge: At the University Press.

Osgood, C. E., G. J. Suci, and P. H. Tannenbaum. 1957. *The Measurement of Meaning.* Urbana: University of Illinois Press.

Otto, Rudolph. 1950. *The Idea of the Holy.* London: Oxford University Press.

Otto, Walter. 1954. *The Homeric Gods: The Spiritual Significance of Greek Religion.* Trans. Modes Hadas. New York: Thames and Hudson.

Outlaw, Lucius T., Jr. 1996. *On Race and Philosophy.* New York: Routledge.

Pagels, Elaine. 1995. *The Origin of Satan.* New York: Random House.

Palmer, Stuart. 1974. "Family Members as Murder Victims." In *Violence in the Family.* Ed. Suzanne Steinmetz and Murray Straus. New York: Harper and Row.

Panofsky, E. 1955. *The Life and Art of Albrecht Dürer.* Princeton, N.J.: Princeton University Press.

Paris, Ginette. 1986. *Pagan Meditations.* Dallas: Spring Publications.

Parke, R., and B. Tinsley. 1981. "The Father's Role in Infancy: Determinants of Involvement in Caregiving and Play." In *The Role of the Father in Child Development.* Ed. Michael E. Lamb. New York: John Wiley and Sons.

Parsons, L. 1991. "The Ball Game in the Southern Pacific Coast Cotzumalhuapa Region and Its Impact on Kaminalijuyu During the Middle Classic." In *The Mesoamerican Ballgame.* Ed. V. L. Scarborough and D. R. Wilcox. Tucson: University of Arizona Press.

Perry, John. 1966. *Lord of the Four Quarters: Myths of the Royal Fathers.* New York: Collier Books.

Pirsig, Robert. 1974. *Zen and the Art of Motorcycle Maintenance: An Inquiry into Values.* New York: Bantam.

Plato. 1961. *The Collected Dialogues of Plato.* Ed. Edith Hamilton and Huntington Cairns. Princeton, N.J.: Princeton University Press.

———. "Catylus." In *The Collected Dialogues of Plato.* Trans. B. Jowett. Ed. Edith Hamilton and Huntington Cairns. Bollingen Series 71. Princeton, N.J.: Princeton University Press.

Plotinus. 1956. *Plotinus: The Eneads.* Trans. Stephen MacKenna. London: Faber and Faber.

Portman, Adolf. 1967. *Animal Forms and Patterns.* New York: Schocken Books.

Qualls, Nancy. 1988. *The Sacred Prostitute: Eternal Aspect of the Feminine.* Toronto: Inner City Books.

Rank, Otto. 1952. *The Trauma of Birth.* New York: R. Brunner.

Reinhold, Meyer. 1976. "The Generation Gap in Antiquity." In *The Conflict of Generations in Ancient Greece and Rome.* Ed. Stephen Bertman. Amsterdam: B. R. Gruner.

Rilke, Rainer Maria. 1967. *Duino Elegies.* (1939) Trans. J. B. Leishman and S. Spender. New York: W. W. Norton.

————. 1982. *The Selected Poetry of Rainer Maria Rilke.* Ed. and trans. Stephen Mitchell. New York: Random House.

————. 1992. "Sometimes a Man Stands up During Supper." Trans. Robert Bly In *The Rag and Bone Shop of the Heart: Poems for Men.* Ed. Robert Bly, James Hillman, and Michael Meade. New York: HarperCollins.

Romanyshyn, Robert. 1989. *Technology as Symptom and Dream.* New York: Routledge.

Rumi. 1992. "The Core of Masculinity." Trans. Coleman Barks. In *The Rag and Bone Shop of the Heart: Poems for Men.* Ed. Robert Bly, James Hillman, and Michael Meade. New York: HarperCollins.

Ruperecht, Carol Schreier. 1974. "The Martial Maid and the Challenge of Androgeny." In *Spring 1974.* New York: Spring Publications.

Ryan, Kelly. 1997. "More Kids in U.S. Die Violently." *Dallas Morning News,* April 15.

Samuels, Andrew. 1989. "Introduction." In *The Father: Contemporary Jungian Perspectives.* New York: New York University Press.

Sandner, Donald. "The Father-Son Relationship." In *Betwixt and Between.* Ed. Louise Carus Mahdi, Steven Foster, and Meredith Little. LaSalle, Ill.: Open Court.

Sardello, Robert. 1992. *Facing the World With Soul.* Hudson, N.Y.: Lindesfarne.

Schlessinger, Arthur, Jr. 1968. *Violence: America in the Sixties.* New York: New American Library.

Schlosser, Eric. 1997, September. "A Grief Like No Other." *The Atlantic Monthly.*

Schwartz, Benjamin. 1997, May. "What Jefferson Helps to Explain." *Atlantic Monthly.*

Schwartz, Regina. 1997. *The Curse of Cain: The Violent Legacy of Monotheism.* Chicago: University of Chicago Press.

Sewell, S., and B. Sewell. 1997, October. "The Feminist View of Domestic Violence vs Scientific Studies." *The Backlash!*

Shacter, Burt, and Jeffrey Seinfeld. 1994. "Personal Violence and the Culture of Violence." *Social Work,* 39(4), 347–50.

Sharp, Deborah. 1996. "Advocates Divided on Anti-pedophile Bill." *USA Today,* May 9.

Sheldrake, Rupert. 1988. *The Presence of the Past: Morphic Resonance and the Habits of Nature.* New York: Random House.

Schele, L. 1986. *The Blood of Kings: Dynasty and Ritual in Mayan Art.* Fort Worth: Kimball Art Museum.

Siegfried, Tom. 1996. "Faulty Premise: Mental Illness' Tie to Violence Exaggerated." *Dallas Morning News,* April 28, J1.

Silberer, Herbert. 1970. *Problems of Mysticism and Its Symbolism.* Trans. Smith Ely Jelliffe. New York: Samuel Weiser.

Slater, Glenn. 2000. "A Psychology of Bullets." The Salt Journal, March/ April, Vol. 2, No. 1.

Smithsonian Institute. Department of Communications. Television display.

Sophocles. 1954. "Oedipus at Colonus." Trans. Robert Fitzgerald. In *Sophocles I.* Ed. David Grene and Richmond Lattimore. Chicago: University of Chicago Press.

———. 1954. "Oedipus the King." Trans. David Grene. In *Sophocles I.* Ed. David Grene and Richmond Lattimore. Chicago: University of Chicago Press.

"Status of Guns." 1995. *Dallas Morning News,* December 31.

Steinmetz, Suzanne, and Murray Straus, eds. 1974. *Violence in the Family.* New York: Harper and Row.

Stevens, Amy. 1993. "Who's Daddy: A Los Angeles Lawyer Specializes in Helping Non-biological Fathers." *The Wall Street Journal,* June 17, 1.

Stevens, Wallace. 1992. "The Irish Cliffs of Moher." In *The Rag and Bone Shop of the Heart: Poems for Men.* Ed. Robert Bly, James Hillman, and Michael Meade. New York: HarperCollins.

Straus, Murray, and Richard Gelles. 1990. *Physical Violence in American Families.* New Brunswick: Transaction.

Tausk, V. 1967. "On the Origin of the 'Influencing Machine' in Schizo-phrenia." In *The Psycho-Analytic Reader.* Ed. R. Fliess. New York: International Universities Press.

Tedlock, D., trans. 1985. *Popol Vuh: The Mayan Book of the Dawn of Life.* New York: Simon and Schuster.

Thomas, Dylan. 1963. "Do Not Go Gentle Into That Good Night." In *Miscellany One.* London: J. M. Dent and Sons.

Thomas, Hugh. 1997. *The Slave Trade: The Story of the Atlantic Slave Trade, 1440–1870.* New York: Simon and Schuster.

Tichi, C. 1991. *Electronic Hearth: Creating an American Television Culture.* New York: Oxford University Press.

Time–Life. 1997. *The Mighty Chieftains.* Alexandria, Va.: Time-Life.

Toobin, Jeffrey. 1997. *The Run of His Life: The People v. O.J. Simpson.* New York: Simon and Schuster.

Todorov, Tzvetan. 1993. *On Human Diversity.* Trans. C. Porter. Cambridge, Mass.: Harvard University Press.

Turner, Victor. 1967. *The Forest of Symbols: Aspects of Ndembu Ritual.* Ithaca, N.Y.: Cornell University Press.

———. 1969. *The Ritual Process.* Ithaca, N.Y.: Cornell University Press.

———. 1983. "Liminal to Liminoid in play, flow and ritual: An essay in comparative symbology." In *Play, Games and Sports in Cultural Contexts.* Ed. J. Harris and R. Park. Champaign: University of Illinois Press.

van Gennep, A. 1960. *Rites of Passage.* Chicago: University of Chicago Press.

Van Soest, Dorothy, and Shirley Bryant. 1995. "The Urban Dilemma: Violence Reconceptualized for Social Work." *Social Work,* 40(4).

Vander Lee, Jana. Article. "Navajo Weaving." Unpublished.

Vergil. 1962. *Vergil's Aeneid.* Trans. L. R. Lind. Bloomington: University of Indiana Press.

Vitale, A. 1973. "The Archetype of Saturn or Transformation of the Father." In *Fathers and Mothers.* Ed. James Hillman et al. Zurich: Spring Publications.

Vogt, Gregory Max. 1991. *Return to Father: Archetypal Dimensions of the Patriarch.* Dallas: Spring Publications.

Wellisch, E. 1954. *Isaac and Oedipus.* London: Routledge and Kegan Paul.

Wheelwright, Phillip. 1964. *Heraclitus.* New York: Atheneum.

Wiesel, Elie. 1976. *Messengers of God: Biblical Portraits and Legends.* Trans. Marion Wiesel. New York: Random House.

Williams, Harry T., ed. 1980. *Selected Writings and Speeches of Abraham Lincoln.* New York: Hendricks House.

Wilmer, H. 1986. "Combat Nightmares." In *Spring 1986.* Dallas: Spring Publications.

Winn, M. 1977. *The Plug-in Drug.* New York: Viking Press.

Winnicott, D. W. 1971. "The Use of an Object and Relating through Identifications" (1969). In *Playing and Reality.* New York: Routledge.

Witherspoon, Gary. 1977. *Language and Art in the Navajo Universe.* Ann Arbor: University of Michigan Press.

Wolkstein, Diane, and Samuel Noah Kramer. 1983. *Inanna: Queen of Heaven and Earth*. New York: Harper and Row.

Wright, Robert. 1995. "The Biology of Violence." *The New Yorker,* March 13.

Zahan, Dominique. 1977. "White, Red and Black: Color Symbolism in Black Africa." In *Color Symbolism: Six Excerpts from the Eranos Yearbook 1972*. Dallas: Spring Publications.

SUBJECT INDEX

aesthetics *(aisthesis)*, 24, 28; Navajo,
    14–18. *See also* beauty, form
alchemy, 52, 66, 68, 83, 89, 96–103;
    calcinatio, 97–98, *coagulatio,* 98;
    solutio, 98. *See also anima mundi,*
    matter, *prima materia,* soul, spirit
alethia, 24, 28
Aphrodite, 23, 26, 29, 57–58
anima mundi, 3, 52, 139–40

beauty, 21–31; as action, 26–28; as being,
    17–18, 29–31; as knowledge, 28–29;
    Navajo, 7–18. *See also* aesthetics,
    form
blackness, 147–150
body, 9, 17, 24–25, 28, 47–48

culture, 3, 12, 15, 17, 38, 83; American and
    violence, 121–24; diseases of, 9, 53,
    54, 139–40; emergence of, 18–19; and
    ethos, 8–9; native and violence,
    127–28; soul of, 51–53; Western and
    violence, 125–26. *See also* Maya,
    Navajo

death, 18, 68, 101, 149; in alchemy,
    96–103; and imagination, 2–4, 30–31,
    140; and marriage, 107–113; as
    metaphor, 2–4; in play, 38–39, 41,
    43–44, 48–49; in relationship, 93–96.
    See also imagination, form, other,
    soul

eidos, 2, 25, 28. *See also* form, image
eros, 94
ethnos, 134, 145–46
ethos, 8–9

face, 3, 29. *See also* form, image
fairy tale, 99–101
form, 157; as pattern of being, 2–3, 9, 13,
    151; as perceptible, 24, 28, 30–31; in
    play, 40, 47–49; and relationship, 94,
    97. *See also* aesthetics, beauty, other

gender: conflict, 152; Navajo, 16; and
    violence, 118, 125–26, 152

head, as symbol, 39–42, 43, 47
ho'zho, 8–11, 14–8

idea, 1–2, 12, 28. *See also* form
image: as encompassing perceiver and
    perceived, 18, 27–28; of father and
    son, 73–74; as larger-than-life form, 3,
    4, 30; in Navajo culture, 11–12; in
    play, 43, 45, 48; as television, 60, 65,
    68. *See also* aesthetic, beauty, form,
    imagination
imagination, 25, 45, 47, 67, 139; as action,
    26–29; as death, 2, 4; as knowledge,
    3; as seeing, 2, 149–50; as violence,
    136. *See also* image
Inanna, 103–113
initiation, 36, 43, 75, 133

177

NAME INDEX